ETHICS

for ADDICTION
PROFESSIONALS

ABOUT THE AUTHORS

LeClair Bissell, M.D., N.C.A.C. II, is a former president of the American Medical Society on Alcoholism (now ASAM) and a lecturer, researcher, and consultant in the addiction field. She has written numerous articles and coauthored several books on chemical dependency and related topics, including *To Care Enough: Intervention with Chemically Dependent Colleagues*, *Chemical Dependency in Nursing: The Deadly Diversion*, and *Alcoholism in the Professions*.

James E. Royce, S.J., Ph.D., is a professor emeritus of psychology and addiction studies at Seattle University. He has been on the board of directors of the National Council on Alcoholism and Drug Dependency since 1976 and received the NCA Marty Mann award for his contributions to public and professional education about alcoholism. His publications include numerous journal articles and the book *Alcohol Problems and Alcoholism: A Comprehensive Survey*.

ETHICS
for ADDICTION PROFESSIONALS

SECOND EDITION

LeClair Bissell, M.D., N.C.A.C. II
James E. Royce, S.J., Ph.D.

With a foreword by Gary Richard Schoener

 HAZELDEN®

Hazelden Educational Materials
Center City, Minnesota 55012-0176

©1987, 1994 by Hazelden Foundation
All rights reserved. Published 1987
Second Edition 1994
Printed in the United States of America
No portion of this publication may be
reproduced in any manner without the
written permission of the publisher

Library of Congress Cataloging in Publication Data
Bissell, LeClair.
   Ethics for addiction professionals / LeClair Bissell, James E. Royce;
with a foreword by Gary Richard Schoener. — 2nd ed.
       p.   cm.
   Includes bibliographical references.
   ISBN: 0-89486-454-8
   1. Alcoholism counselors—Professional ethics—United States.
   2. Drug abuse counselors—Professional ethics—United States.
   3. Allied health professionals—Professional ethics—United States.
   I. Royce, James E. II. Title.
   HV5279.B57 1994
   174' .9362—dc20   94-32433
                                                              CIP

Editor's note
Hazelden Educational Materials offers a variety of information on chemical dependency and related areas. Our publications do not necessarily
represent Hazelden's programs, nor do they officially speak for any Twelve
Step organization.

The typeface used in this book is Goudy.

CONTENTS

GARY RICHARD SCHOENER

FOREWORD

The addiction field has been evolving as a profession for a number of decades. Originally, counselors were seen as paraprofessionals who helped their clients by providing support and sharing personal experiences. Early training programs, such as the one at the University of Minnesota, largely served those who had been through chemical dependency treatment or had been members of Alcoholics Anonymous. Later, addictions counselors were seen as members of a recovery program rather than independent professionals who needed more than the rules of the program to make decisions about care, release of records, and other complex concerns.

During the past few years, with the advent of licensure in a number of states, as well as evolving legal standards for professional responsibility in both statutes and case law, the addictions field has clearly become an independent profession. Furthermore, with the growth of health maintenance organizations (HMOs) and the expansion of professional standards review by indemnity insurance carriers, such as Blue Cross/Blue Shield, the work of addiction counselors faces increasing review by outside parties. Treatment decisions are being more greatly affected by outside forces and are under greater scrutiny. In this context, *Ethics for Addiction Professionals* by LeClair Bissell, M.D., N.C.A.C. II, and James E. Royce, S.J., Ph.D., has become essential reading for people at all levels of treatment work, from administration to counseling.

Those who provide addiction intervention and treatment services come, as the authors note, from a wide range of fields and traditions. Some come from fields with a long history of ethical standards and codes, while others bring with them commitment to help others based on their own experiences in recovery. This book speaks eloquently to the diversity in this field, which is, on one hand, an amalgam of many other fields and traditions and, on the other hand, something quite unique.

Among the national changes affecting this field, as well as much of the American workplace, the Americans with Disabilities Act (ADA) has had an impact on how employees with addiction problems should be treated. Bissell and Royce examine the issue of the counselor in relapse with this standard in mind, but also note that a relapse is a serious event for the program and the clients because the counselor represents a role model. The authors courageously advise candor with clients about counselor breakdowns—something with which I completely agree.

In discussing professional competence, the authors note the A.A. tradition of cooperation without affiliation, advising counselors to know their limits and to seek appropriate continuing professional education to expand skills and update knowledge. They examine the problems that may occur when counselors and programs with experience in working with adults expand their work to cover adolescents; the authors emphasize that work with young people has become a speciality of its own. They also warn against encroaching on the expertise of physicians by advising clients to stop taking various medications.

Client rights are discussed in the light of the "myth of choice." The authors note that many so-called voluntary clients are coming in for help in response to considerable pressure, and that third-party payers, employers, and even counselors may push particular treatment options. The authors recommend that the client be offered a choice of treatment options, so if the client enters treatment, he or she can at least choose which program to enter.

This book also offers an excellent discussion of the child abuse reporting issue. The authors correctly note that for more than a decade there was a raging debate about whether client confidentiality guidelines in addictions programs, which are based on federal statutes, outweighed state statutes requiring reporting. The authors discuss the federal legislation that clarified this issue and examine the current standards in the field.

The authors discuss in some detail one of the unique and most challenging problems in the field: the fact that recovering professionals may end up being in the same A.A. or support group as their "clients." Refreshingly, the authors do not fret over this reality and simply note that contact in A.A. is inevitable. They provide excellent, practical advice on how to handle this situation, after first cautioning the professional to remember the different roles of treatment and A.A. groups. Bissell and Royce write that problems can be avoided if the professional avoids scheduling appointments with former clients and avoids being alone with them.

The authors discuss sexual and romantic involvements with former clients. After reviewing the arguments, they advise against such relationships for a number of reasons.

There is also an excellent discussion of the economic pressures that addiction professionals and programs face. The authors examine a number of ethical dilemmas brought about by an environment that values cost containment in the short run above all else. In examining the pressures to engage in diagnostic subterfuge for monetary reasons, Bissell and Royce provide a forum for frank discussion of issues that we would prefer to pretend do not influence our judgments.

This book concludes with two useful resources: a bibliography of key reading materials and a sample ethics code. The sample code will be of great value to professionals and programs seeking to develop standards. It covers a broad range of ethical principles and provides concrete standards relative to many of the dilemmas discussed in the book. Those seeking to develop their own code will find this a useful starting place.

The wise counselor or administrator will not wait for licensure or for a professional organization to set up standards. He or she will take a proactive stance and help develop standards for programs and professionals. Treatment dilemmas occur every day; they cannot await the legislature, court decisions, or even committee meetings. An addictions professional must be just that: a professional who is focused both on client care and on how the field is seen by the public and by other professionals.

Between 400 and 500 B.C. Hippocrates wrote his physician's oath. Beyond its specific standards, it is noteworthy for its overall charge: "With holiness and purity I will practise my art. . . . in to whatever houses I go, I go for the benefit of the sick, voluntarily abstaining from acts of mischief and corruption. . . ." Bissell and Royce expect no less from addictions professionals and provide guidance on reaching such high aspirations.

Licensed Psychologist and
Executive Director
Walk-In Counseling Center
Minneapolis, Minnesota

GARY RICHARD SCHOENER

LECLAIR BISSELL

PREFACE

Some years ago I was asked to serve on the ethics committee of the Association of Labor-Management Administrators and Consultants of Alcoholism, Inc. (now Employee Assistance Professionals Association). At that time, a code of ethics was in place, but the problems involved in getting members to abide by it were just beginning to surface.

My own background and training were limited to a course in ethics given in 1949 at the University of Colorado and one or two single lectures during my medical school years. I had read and recited the Hippocratic oath and enjoyed its flavor of tradition and antiquity. I had also read and not enjoyed the American Medical Association (AMA) code of ethics, which struck me as being more concerned with economics than with the welfare of patients.

I had the additional experience of attempting, along with other staff, to agree on a code of ethics for a residential treatment facility. It was apparent, even then, that we were being heavily influenced by fear of possible malpractice suits and by the need to meet accreditation standards. We had to make a conscious effort to keep those fears separate from the need to make ethical decisions based on what was beneficial for the patient. Setting our own standards was desirable but not easy. If anyone else had attempted to spell them out for our particular kind of treatment setting, I was unable to locate them.

Then in 1979 I was asked to speak on ethics in counseling at the Southeastern Conference on Alcohol and Drug Abuse (SECAD). In preparation I asked many people about their experiences, problems, and concerns. Most were eager for discussion and many were generous about providing examples of difficulties or bringing questions to my attention. My presentation was a patchwork of what they told me. I had expected people to be interested because the material itself was intriguing, but the level of interest was much higher than I could have predicted. I was surprised; none of this was really news.

What people said was that although this was not the first time they had been aware of, or concerned about, ethical issues, they felt that the presentation of the issues was new. As one person put it, "Somebody finally said it! Now maybe we can begin to talk about it."

This book represents an attempt to go on with the discussion.

JAMES E. ROYCE

PREFACE

Specialists in treating alcohol and other drug addictions are developing a new profession, and a code of ethics is one mark of a profession. Being in a young field, we need to develop a tradition of professional conduct. This is the first major attempt, to our knowledge, to spell it out in detail.

Since much of this is pioneer territory, my co-author, LeClair Bissell, and I are both aware that this book attempts not to give final answers but to ask the right questions. We have recognized a need and a desire for more discussion and information on professional ethics among both trainees and experienced professionals in the addiction field. Ethics ranked at the top of a 1986 professional development and training needs-assessment survey report among employee assistance program (EAP) managers. Now, practically all states are requiring some hours or course credits in ethics as a condition of certification or recertification as a counselor in alcoholism or other drug addiction.

The co-author of this book, LeClair Bissell—a certified alcoholism counselor (C.A.C. and N.C.A.C. II), a physician, a former president of the American Medical Society on Alcoholism, as well as chair of its ad hoc committee on ethics—has for many years had the opportunity to observe professional behavior nationwide. Added to this is her courage in speaking out on sensitive issues where many of us might be tempted to take a softer approach.

I am a psychologist who has been teaching in the Addiction Studies Program at Seattle University since 1950. I have been counseling chemically dependent people and their spouses since before that time and have taught medical ethics. As co-chairman of the Washington state committee I wrote the final draft on norms for certification of alcoholism counselors which became the working-paper of the 1974 National Institute on Alcohol Abuse and Alcoholism Littlejohn Board, the first national effort at credentialing. I have served since 1976 on the board of directors of the National Council on Alcoholism and Drug Dependence. As three-time licensing board chairman, I administered our state psychology ethics code and was elected president and later a fellow of the American Association of State Psychology Boards.

The use of the word *addiction* in the title of this book reflects the fact that although alcohol is a major problem drug in America, poly-drug use is so widespread that most professionals and treatment centers must address it. Also, recent progress in the biochemistry of neuroregulators and receptor sites in the brain suggests intimate relations between the actions of alcohol and other drugs. The terms *alcohol and other drug dependencies* and *chemical dependency* are used interchangeably throughout the book to refer to all addictions. The occasional singling out of alcohol from other drug dependencies reflects the belief that although treatment and recovery issues remain generally the same for all chemical addictions, alcohol continues to be the major problem drug in the United States, exceeded only by tobacco.

Our hope is that if all addiction professionals, both old and new, find food for thought in this book, our professional world will be a better place in which to work and live.

CHAPTER ONE

THE WORKER

A NEW PROFESSION

What is a professional? The dictionary defines a profession as a group of people who share a common body of knowledge, a code of ethics, and a concern for their peers. If ethics are essential to being professional, what are ethics? Again, the dictionary says that ethics comprise the principles of morality, including both the science of the good and the nature of the right, and that they constitute the rules of conduct in respect to a particular class of human actions, such as medical ethics. In health care, law, and social work, and among the clergy, the primary purpose of a code of ethics is to guide professionals in helping clients and their families while behaving in a fair and decent way to colleagues. It is important to abide by the ancient dictum *primum non nocere*, or "first of all, do no harm," yet it is also important to acknowledge that one can harm not only by acting, but by failing to act.

Whether or not a given behavior is legal or illegal does not determine whether or not it is ethical. There are good laws and bad laws. Sometimes the courts are able to render justice, at other times they cannot. For instance, physicians attempting to protect themselves from malpractice suits may sometimes perform unnecessary procedures. Addiction professionals may feel torn between the need to protect themselves or their institution from litigation and the desire to spare a patient unneeded discomfort or expense.

Ethics is not religion, nor statistics on what most people do, nor a trade-union agreement to stop treatment providers from stealing patients from one another. *Ethics is the science of right moral conduct derived from an analysis of human nature by the light of reason.*

Professionals are expected by the general public and by members of other professions to have high standards, to be responsible for their own colleagues, and to act with integrity. A simple definition of ethics might be "the habit of moral courage." If workers resent being called paraprofessionals, a term the authors deplore, and if they are serious about being truly professional, they must build a tradition of acting as professionals in their own right.

In athletics, the major difference between the amateur and the professional is that the latter is paid. In social and health services, while a very few professionals are more interested in money than in helping people, the major difference between a business and a profession is that the business is frankly and primarily aimed at making money, whereas a profession is primarily aimed at rendering service. The true professional does not work for a boss or for dollars, but for the purpose of serving the patient. A professional has a genuine concern that disadvantaged people also receive services. Success is not measured in profit, but in quality of service. Some of the noblest professions are the least lucrative. The payoff is measured in personal satisfaction and in the joy, awe, and privilege of sharing human lives and secrets.

UNIQUE CONSIDERATIONS OF THE CHEMICAL DEPENDENCY FIELD

Workers in the field of alcoholism and other drug dependencies have much in common with other helping professions, particularly those in health care. There are, in addition, some unique considerations where one cannot simply borrow from the experience of others. There are differences and they require discussion.

One unique difference stems from the fact that many workers in this field have themselves recovered from the same illness from which they are helping others to recover. For many years alcohol and other drug dependencies were regarded not as legitimate illnesses, but as signs of weakness or moral problems. Those afflicted by addiction were labeled as suffering from character disorders. Having experienced chemical dependency does not guarantee immunity to any other illness, mental or physical, and no single personality type is either fated to develop a problem or sure to avoid it. Some chemically dependent people suffer from character disorders, but the vast majority do not. As a matter of fact, most suffer from an exquisitely well developed sense of guilt.

The Twelve Steps of Alcoholics Anonymous provide for a moral inventory, a discussion of character defects with someone else, an attempt at restitution, and an ongoing effort at self-monitoring. Why? Because when one can neither approve of one's own actions nor rationalize them away, there is usually a nagging sense of inner discomfort. An alcoholic or other drug addict knows all too well how to make unpleasant feelings subside, at least for the time being. If negative feelings last too long or grow too strong, the temptation to reach for a drink or another drug may be too great to resist. As a result—even though chemical dependency is a disease and not a moral problem—to remain abstinent the addict may need to behave in a manner that is "more moral" than what is good enough for the rest of the world. Excessive guilt poses a real danger if allowed to build. A well-considered code of ethics, both professional and personal, can be a source of inner strength and confidence.

CREDENTIALS

Chemical dependency counselors come from a variety of backgrounds and bring with them a wide array of credentials. Many enter the field from social work, psychology, psychiatric nursing, or medicine. Unfortunately, most professional schools, even those with the finest of reputations, cannot be relied on to teach their graduates about chemical dependency, and sometimes what they do offer is inaccurate. This seems to stem from a basic failure to appreciate that there is a specialized body of knowledge professionals should possess to work effectively in this field. When a school does not acknowledge that this vital information exists, students are not aware that they should attempt to gain it.

A physician or nurse who would never dream of working in a coronary care unit without adequate schooling will plunge into the business of giving advice or medications to an addicted person with hardly a second thought. Unfortunately, since these professionals are perceived as authorities by both patient and family, their mistakes can be hard to correct. The additional background these professionals have does prove extremely useful once the other specialized material has been learned. One of the reasons many people have earned certification as counselors and list the C.A.C. or equivalent credential after the M.D., R.N., Ph.D., or M.S.W. is to alert others to the fact that holding a degree other than certification in the addiction field says nothing about one's ability to do this specific work.

The counselor who has earned certification in a specialized academic chemical dependency program, or who lacks a degree, may have quite a different problem. In the 1970s when federal money became available for chemical dependency training, colleges and universities rushed to develop courses in alcoholism counseling, frequently at a master's degree level. These were often a combination of parts of preexisting courses borrowed from other disciplines, plus some additional practical experience working in a chemical dependency agency. Because these were new and unfamiliar degrees, those hiring the graduates were unsure of how much or little they were taught or were prepared to do. While some of this material was excellent, a code of ethics was almost never addressed. Most colleges and states now require a course in ethics for addiction professionals.

In a still more unsettled position is the counselor whose major qualification is personal recovery from alcoholism or another drug dependency. As a wise manager of a women's halfway house once said, "Just because you had your appendix out doesn't qualify you to take out mine. It may get you interested, but that's all." Just as a professional from another discipline must be schooled in chemical dependency counseling, so too a counselor with personal chemical dependency experience has much to learn. The former will be able to take advantage of previous training, while the latter will have the ability to function as a role model of successful recovery, as well as know how suffering from chemical dependency can feel. These are different strengths which can be used in a complementary fashion to help a patient, or which can lead to competition between the recovered and the nonrecovered professional (Krystal and Moore 1963, Lemere 1964).

The reader will note that the authors say *recovered*, following the wording of the Big Book, *Alcoholics Anonymous*. Here *recovered* does not mean "cured" in the sense that chemically dependent people will never use alcohol or other mood-altering drugs again. For this reason some prefer the term *recovering*, to remind themselves they must always avoid that first drink or other drug. However, A.A. *Guidelines* warns members not to use the term *recovering* outside the fellowship, lest it be misunderstood to mean the person is still using (Royce 1986). As National Council on Alcoholism founder Marty Mann said at a conference in Salt Lake City in 1976, *recovering* to an outsider means that A.A. doesn't work, that after thirty-seven years she still had not recovered, that she was still sick. Growth is a sign of health; life is not static, so progress rather than perfection remains a goal for recovered alcoholics. *Recovering* is an appropriate term in early stages of remission where mere abstinence is not proof of genuine sobriety or stable recovery.

The authors use *patient* and *client* interchangeably, aware that consistency demands that if chemical dependency is called a disease, then its victims are patients.

In one regard, chemical dependency counselors are in the unique position of belonging to a profession dedicated to treating just one specific type of illness. Physicians and nurses are expected to care for a variety of illnesses, but addiction counselors are in the strange position of being expected to understand how to treat addictive disease but not other things. Unfortunately, human problems refuse to stay neatly pigeonholed, so a host of other issues immediately arise. If counselors deal only with alcohol and other drugs, they risk being called narrow, limited, and rigid. If they lean too far the other way, the outcry, though different, is just as loud (Keller 1975).

The ability to serve as a role model is the one and only thing the successfully recovered person can offer that no one else can. If liked, accepted, and admired, such a person can be believed and imitated, and can offer hope and reassurance that a life entirely free of chemical supports can be rich and fulfilling. Recovered people have credentials that include not only what they know, but where they have been and what changes they have made. Such credentials are powerful but may present a two-edged sword. How is the quality of a good role model judged? What is the quality or quantity of sobriety or abstinence, or of family recovery, to be required? A.A. *Guidelines: For A.A. Members Employed in the Alcoholism Field* suggests that A.A. members have three to five years of abstinence before working in the field. The authors believe that at least three years of continuous sobriety and abstinence from other mood-altering drugs is essential.

LEVEL OF EXPERIENCE

The field has been plagued with individuals who, after being abstinent for only a few weeks, present themselves as qualified to advise others. Treatment agencies may be all too willing to hire and exploit these people. Their salary demands are often low since they may not be employable elsewhere, their good intentions are quite genuine, and their level of energy and dedication is high. The would-be employer may be tempted to hire such a person in order to offer a safe environment (what could be called a form of extended treatment), but this involves tremendous risk. It is hard to pass on to others what we have not yet learned for ourselves, and recovering people who cannot function except by working in the field of their own illness are extremely limited, both in terms of personal recovery and in the quality of counseling they are able to offer. This may be denied, and many anecdotes may be served up to illustrate the virtues of leaping immediately from patient to therapist status, but a sheltered workshop for a person not yet entirely well is just that.

If working with other chemically dependent people is the right career choice for an individual, it will remain so after a period of consideration and training, and after some work experience and personal recovery in the outside world. It pays to consider carefully the real reasons for all the rush (Birch and Davis Associates 1986, Staub and Kent 1973, Valle 1979). It should be obvious that it is unethical to claim qualifications we do not possess just because we are in the process of acquiring them.

The human qualities needed to counsel chemically dependent people and their families are essentially the same as for counseling people with other problems: the appropriate knowledge base, openness, realistic empathy, personal warmth, and a great deal of self-awareness. The very success of A.A. and other Twelve Step groups, and the impressive performance of their members who have entered the counseling field, has led to a great deal of respect for their efforts. Unfortunately, many outsiders are unable to distinguish between the mature and competent recovered person with good quality sobriety and the persuasive, attractive con artist. Those who have had experience running treatment agencies will share war stories of staff they have hired, ending their recital with a plea that for the sake of patients and everyone else concerned, references be requested and meticulously checked before any prospective employee is authorized to treat others. An attractive candidate who seems the least likely to need investigation may be the very person who needs it most.

Some of the people most impatient to start treating others and least likely to question their ability or qualifications are people who have already been working as professionals in a health care field and are newly recovered. Already accustomed to seeing themselves, and being seen, as experts, their new insights and personal knowledge seem to be all they need and in they plunge. In a field often short of qualified professionals they are frequently seen as a miraculous solution to a personnel problem and are welcomed with open arms. Sometimes this works, but interest alone does not mean ability, nor does the experience of personal recovery. Counseling chemically dependent people involves skills and aptitudes that may or may not be there, regardless of good intentions. While a lay person is usually carefully screened and may be refused a position, no such constraints (or lack of credentials) may slow the newly recovered and eager psychologist or physician who is today's patient and decides to be tomorrow's expert.

If we have had a family member with an alcohol or other drug problem, it is just as important to have dealt with that as thoroughly as if we had faced such a problem ourselves. Recovered people can at least use a dry date as a partial measure of success, even if it came many months after treatment or regular attendance in a Twelve Step group. But how do we set even that crude a measure for the spouse who may have had years of marital counseling and Al-Anon attendance before beginning to sense what either was all about? We owe it to our patients and to ourselves to determine whether we are entering this field for the patients' well-being or to find personal answers. We may find our motives are mixed. If so, that does not mean we must avoid the field, but we had best be fully aware of the hazards and have skilled supervision in facing them.

DISCRIMINATION

America is very conscious of laws and traditions regarding discrimination due to race, creed, national origin, color, age, gender, or sexual orientation. Alcoholism and other drug addictions are disabilities protected from discrimination under the Americans with Disabilities Act. One cannot be denied employment or dismissed simply for being chemically dependent if otherwise properly qualified, but that does not mean one cannot be dismissed for poor job performance resulting from active chemical dependency.

Recovered people sometimes practice a reverse discrimination on the basis of how bad the consequences of drug use became. We'll hear, "He got his sobriety between clean sheets," meaning that this person does not deserve the same consideration as one who slept under bridges. This form of discrimination can be directed toward both recovered and nonrecovered people. Sometimes it's "high bottom" versus "low bottom," with what verges on anger directed at the person who comes seeking sobriety without first having suffered enough.

Is the ability to model quality sobriety a legitimate job qualification or discrimination against those who have not had to face recovery? There are both advantages and disadvantages in the counselor's being a recovered addict. The better facilities seem to favor a mix of recovered people and other professionals as the preferred staffing pattern, giving some preference to those who are recovered, provided they have chemical dependency counseling credentials.

Tradition Eight says that "Alcoholics Anonymous should remain forever nonprofessional," but this does not preclude individual members from becoming professionals. Some unwritten A.A. traditions suggest that members who are also professionals never be sponsors for their own patients or chair A.A. meetings in the treatment facility where they are employed. This latter practice could easily confuse patients as to the distinct roles of treatment and A.A.

THE COUNSELOR IN RELAPSE

A particularly hard problem to face is that of counselors or other addiction professionals who relapse, and relapse they do (Bissell and Haberman 1984). As of that moment the credential of successful role model is lost. The counselor may be supporting a family and have few qualifications to do other kinds of work. Who will take over the case load? Suppose the relapse is not into drinking or hard drug use but a more subtle matter of using other, seemingly less dangerous drugs?

Isn't it inconsistent to advocate employee assistance programs, insisting that chemical dependency is a disease, only to immediately dismiss a professional who relapses? The employer knows that the illness is there and that a certain number of relapses are entirely possible, as in any chronic illness. This is a point on which we have an obligation to educate the public as well as professionals, in this instance by the example of our own behavior.

What will the patients be told? Will they be lied to after all that may have been said about openness and honesty? If we choose candor, is it fair to ask a patient to accept treatment from someone fresh from a relapse? We often advise others to stick with the winners: can we ask patients to accept a group leader who has not been winning? None of this has dealt with the fact that this person in relapse is very much like us, with all our common humanity and vulnerability. Yet decide we must, and it will rarely be easy.

If an institution is large enough, the person in relapse can be offered another position that does not involve patient contact. In a halfway house with four staff members, that option doesn't exist. In a large treatment community where residents and staff progress by stages from new arrival to staff status, demotion without separation is a possibility. Most facilities will have to make a more black-or-white, go-or-stay decision.

Since this problem will arise sooner or later, it should be discussed before it happens so employees know what to expect and management knows what action to take. Ideally, this policy should be made known to new staff when they are hired so decisions are not made in the heat of crisis and staff are not quarreling among themselves over what should be done.

Whatever policy is adopted, it will have profound effect on the running of the institution and on staff and patient morale. No matter what is decided, it will have certain no-win elements and there will rarely be full agreement among all parties when a relapse happens. The distress can be held to a minimum if there has been thoughtful planning.

If an initial job requirement is at least two years of recovery and that is violated, reality dictates that the employee not be rehired until that time has passed. There is no way to speed the passage of time. In other professions, a license may be withheld for arbitrary and even ridiculously long periods. If addiction counselors are to claim the benefits of being seen as professionals, some of the limitations must be accepted as well.

DRINKING AND OTHER DRUG USE

Even more difficult may be the problem presented by the person who does not have a previous history of chemical dependency but who develops a dependency while working in the addiction field (West 1988). There may have been no conscious awareness that trouble was on the way, although there is the possibility that an awareness of one's own addictive tendencies may account for an interest in the field. Chemical dependency may not be contagious, but it often looks that way. Again, there are no easy answers, but staff should be clear about what is regarded as appropriate personal use of alcohol and other drugs and what the consequences will be if policy is disregarded. If staff complain that private life is just that and not the concern of the employer or colleague, it is quite fair to reply that in this particular field, the use of chemicals and one's belief system about them are job related. If one is convinced that the answer to human problems is chemical use, it is hard to see how that conviction can be left at home. The time to settle these questions is before, not after the person is hired.

CHAPTER TWO

COMPETENCE

AREAS AND LIMITS

One of the most common and most difficult problems, faced almost daily, is the question of individual competence. Not everyone is able to do everything, but where are the limits? They continue to elude us no matter how hard we work at policies and definitions, because they change with setting, time, individual talents, and personalities. Many skills can be learned. Others perhaps never can be. A hard look at some of the problems may help us avoid a number of pitfalls and make us more aware of and comfortable with our limitations. We can try for the wisdom to see the difference between what to accept as within our abilities and what to refuse as beyond our present abilities.

The environment in which counseling is done and the availability of supporting professionals, such as clergy, psychologists, or fellow addiction counselors, create different demands and expectations for both patient and counselor. In many parts of the country there still may be no legal constraint on alcoholism counselors, whether credentialed or not, that prevents them from setting up a private practice. The counselor who has been working in a clinic as part of a treatment team and has had regular supervision, immediate access to a physician in case of emergency, a skilled social worker at hand, and other help easily available, may now try to fulfill all of these functions alone. The counselor is the same, the patient the same, but the situation very different. One person who was providing this form of treatment was very hurt when questioned. "Don't you trust me?" she said. "I'm seeing Dr. Brown every week and paying him for supervision!" She was, but the answer was no.

To trust her genuine good intentions was easy. To be comfortable about the situation was another matter. Private practice requires far greater competence and professional training than working in a team under supervision, according to the ethical codes of all professions. Along with specialized training in chemical dependency counseling, a master's degree should be the minimum legal requirement for private practice.

Failure to provide an adequate follow-up plan upon discharge seems an obvious breach of ethical practice. But more subtle problems arise as patients get further into recovery. Many counselors are excellent at breaking down a new patient's denial and helping the patient accept that he or she is chemically dependent, that abstinence must be the goal, and that recovery is possible. The patient moves smoothly into an appropriate mutual-help group and learns new coping skills. He or she begins attending a therapy group and becomes increasingly confident and comfortable with living sober.

It seems like a success story, but six months later things are far from rosy. The tasks of early sobriety are quite different from those faced later on. When the novelty has worn off, when abstinence alone has failed to rejuvenate a mediocre marriage, when a major decision about a job change needs to be made, when parenting an upset adolescent seems hardly worth the effort, when sexual functioning has still not been fully restored, and when, in general, the rewards of sobriety seem like a broken promise, patient and counselor may discover that they are no longer right for each other. The treatment and guidance needed now may call for a different set of skills. The patient is the same, the counselor is the same, the treatment setting is the same, but the problem is different. The competence needed now is not necessarily greater, but it is not the same.

Sometimes it should be obvious that counselors are being asked to undertake problems beyond their abilities. It is important that after years of neglect family systems in alcoholic families are finally receiving attention. But does it make sense to ask a counselor whose only expertise at marriage counseling may be derived from the misery of his or her own three failed marriages, or a counselor who visited Al-Anon a few times, to assume the role of family therapist? This happens too frequently, and the result is that the needs of the family are sacrificed on the altar of getting the addicted family member into recovery, no matter what the price.

Sometimes counselors deal with their personal prejudices and other limitations by denying that problems exist. One counselor, when asked about his management of a client's severe anxiety over failure in sexual performance, was eager to explain that it was too early in sobriety to discuss the problem, and that time and physical healing would automatically resolve the difficulty. End of problem, at least for the therapist.

Another counselor was asked how many gay and lesbian clients she had seen in a clinic in the last year and how many of her colleagues were homosexual. Answer: one patient, no fellow staff. At least twenty percent of both groups were easily identifiable by a sophisticated observer as homosexual, but this counselor denied any need for additional training in how to identify or work with this population. Ignorance not only makes a good chaperone, it works well to keep a variety of problems at bay. Discomfort with other races and ethnic groups? Problems relating to the adolescent or to the elderly woman with the weak hearing-aid battery? Uneasiness with the retarded, the handicapped, the cross-addicted, the patient who also has cancer or acquired immune deficiency syndrome (AIDS)? Anger with someone who is merely ugly or disagreeable, or who repeatedly relapses after getting us to believe that this time we had worked the miracle?

No one is comfortable with every group, or sensitive to or even informed about its needs. At best, we need to be aware of what we can and cannot do, and assume responsibility for getting patients we can't help into the best situation available for their particular needs. The real failure is denying there is a problem, thus leaving the problem unresolved and preventing patients from getting help that may be available from someone else.

ASKING FOR ASSISTANCE

Part of the professional obligation of restricting practice to one's area of training and competence is the importance of making referrals to other agencies for services one cannot, or chooses not to, offer. The temptation is to want to handle everything alone. A real expert knows when to ask for help and where to get it. A.A. itself has a long and strong tradition of cooperation without affiliation with various professions. (See A.A. sources in the Bibliography.)

One social worker remarked on the irony that while chemical dependency workers often complain that social workers do not refer to them, she had considerable expertise in handling problems that addiction counselors were untrained for, yet she never got a referral from them. Clergy and psychotherapists, in the past, may have left a bad taste in the recovering person's mouth, but recovered people now acting as counselors need to identify nonaddiction issues and remember that referral is a two-way street. One recent research paper shows that 91 percent of patients complain that their spiritual needs are not adequately met in treatment centers, and a 1983 three-year study of 441 patients called the spiritual "the most neglected part of therapy." This implies an ethical obligation on the part of those responsible for treatment. (On cooperation with clergy, see Apthorp 1985.)

Too often the emphasis on addiction to alcohol or other drugs as the primary problem has created the impression that it is the only problem. Mere removal of the drug doesn't mean family and other problems are resolved. We know that with sobriety a host of new problems that were masked or ignored during drug use often surface. These new problems may need medical, legal, spiritual, marital, vocational, financial, or other types of help. One loyal A.A. member, now a competent professional, remarked at a national meeting of A.A. members working as addiction professionals that if a person had appendicitis, we would not suggest, "Go to more meetings!"

DUAL DIAGNOSIS

It hardly needs saying that both a nonphysician counselor and an A.A. member go beyond their competence when they advise an alcoholic not to take medicine prescribed by a physician. This is practicing medicine without a license and may amount to murder if the addict dies as a result. We are not speaking here of the addictive psychoactive drugs such as amphetamines, barbiturates, opiates, or benzodiazepines, which carry an inherent danger of substitute addiction or synergism, and which often are incorrectly used, whether by prescription or not, to treat addiction. Use of such drugs should always be questioned. We are speaking of other legitimate drugs which may be necessary for addicts who have other medical or psychiatric conditions: digitalis for a heart patient, insulin or oral hypoglycemics for a diabetic, Dilantin for an epileptic, or lithium for a manic-depressive. The same applies to disulfiram (Antabuse) or naltrexone (Trexan), which are not psychoactive drugs or a substitute for alcohol or opiates, and which may be lifesaving for some alcoholics and addicts.

Dual diagnosis, not dual addiction to alcohol and another drug but the occurrence of both addiction and mental illness in the same patient, has in the last decade become increasingly recognized. This presents no really new ethical problems, but it alerts all to the obligation that both addiction and mental health professionals have to cooperate, respect each other's areas of competence, and not go beyond their own. Addiction workers have struggled to get addiction to alcohol and other drugs recognized as a primary illness, not merely the symptom of mental disorder. "You can't do psychotherapy with a toxic brain" became almost a battle cry. There was great effort to determine which came first and which should be treated first.

It is not our place to lay down rules about diagnosis or treatment. But we all have an ethical duty to lay aside territorial jealousies, to admit their limitations, and to cooperate for the good of the patient. Although a licensed psychologist, one co-author of this book readily admits that most psychologists really do not understand addiction. And even well-trained addiction counselors are generally not competent to diagnose and treat mental disorders. Inappropriate response to a suicide threat can have legal as well as human and ethical implications.

There seems to be a greater proportion now of counselors who have college degrees and training in fields other than addictions, such as psychology. Given the current emphasis on dual diagnosis, this seems like a clear plus. But there are dangers.

For one, these newcomers and others may be tempted to look down on older counselors whose qualifications are rooted in recovery, A.A., and nondegree counselor training programs. Some states have proposed legislation that would require counselors to possess certain academic degrees. The reason appears to be primarily economic and political, since these new requirements do not insist on any specific expertise in chemical dependency. One Southern state, for example, specifically exempts the clergy from any need to demonstrate understanding of addiction.

Discounting the experience of older counselors, however, would be both unprofessional and a great loss to the newcomers themselves. Not only are these veterans the ones who built the profession in the first place, but there is much accumulated wisdom in their background and experience and in A.A.'s conference-approved literature. Again, too much emphasis on psychology can cause professionals to miss the basic neurophysiology which underlies addiction, while too much emphasis on degrees can cause administrators to undervalue addiction-specific training and experience.

On the other hand, counselors of the old school are too prone to take a dog-in-the-manger attitude toward the very real contributions that psychology can make to enhance the long-term effectiveness of their efforts. Recent work on relapse prevention is fairly well known, but other approaches have been avoided through either ignorance or prejudice, because these approaches are linked to controlled drinking rather than total abstinence as a goal for recovering persons. This reluctance to be open to new approaches is both unprofessional and unethical, because it robs patients of optimum chances of recovery.

Ignorance about the legal implications of certain actions and court procedures, of how to write a presentence recommendation, and of how to cooperate with probation and parole officers, not only can make a counselor ineffective or harmful, but can also discredit the profession by making its members seem inept. Likewise deplorable is the tendency among some counselors to act as enablers by helping alcoholics or other addicts dodge legal responsibility for their actions, or to generalize and automatically see every person arrested for drunk driving as an alcoholic.

RESPONSIBILITIES OF PATIENTS AND PROFESSIONALS

Some counselors seem to forget that calling chemical dependency a disease does not mean throwing all moral responsibility out the window. The psychologist Lewis M. Andrews, Ph.D., has vividly exposed the myth of "value-free therapy" and depicts the rebirth of ethical values in counseling (Andrews 1987). The patient may not be responsible for being chemically dependent, but still has an obligation to do something about it. Since the very nature of the illness diminishes freedom of choice, the initial obligation may be to listen to others with openness, to accept help, and to use the available means to avoid using alcohol or other drugs. And one may still have some responsibility for the consequences of active addiction, although here guilt must not be confused with regret.

The counselor may have to point out that people may be legally responsible for crimes committed under the influence, even in a blackout, although the degree of guilt is a matter for courts to decide based on the evidence. At times the counselor may have an ethical obligation to confront the patient about responsibility for the consequences of addiction, such as abuse of a spouse or child. One recovered former child abuser told his counselor, "My last few counselors spent hours on understanding why I act that way, but you are the first one who ever told me not to do it." (For a fuller discussion of these issues see Royce 1989, chapter 19.)

The basic principle of not attempting to work beyond one's ability applies to institutions as well as to individuals. For instance, there is a current trend among well-regarded adult treatment programs to claim they have a treatment program for adolescents when they have neither acquired the specially trained staff necessary nor developed the specific types of programs adolescents need. This is unethical. The same holds true for any unqualified facility that treats a significant number of any minority group: African Americans, Jews, gay men and lesbians, American Indians, and so on. Admitting the occasional one or two without added programs or staff may be justified, but admitting a large number or advertising competence in handling special-interest groups leads to an obligation to keep the implied promise and provide appropriate treatment.

Some treatment facilities, usually residential, that were initially designed to treat chemical dependency have moved far beyond their initial mandate. First they added programs for immediate family and significant others of patients. Then they moved into treatment of adult children of alcoholics. Next came gambling and eating disorders. More recently they added codependency, defined as coming from virtually any kind of dysfunctional family. Most recently, sexual addiction is being included. Most of these conditions are regarded as "addictions" of sorts and introduction to Twelve Step programs is seen as part of the cure. While these activities may indeed help some people, there is much room for questions. Is the motive largely financial? The prices charged tend to be very high while evidence of their effectiveness is largely anecdotal. More important, the counselors working in such a facility are very likely to be faced with patients whose problems are well beyond their own experience or training.

PROFESSIONAL DEVELOPMENT

Lastly, competence in a rapidly changing and highly complex field demands constant upgrading of skills and knowledge. Most professions require continuing education as a condition for renewing a license or certification. In-service training is usually not acceptable to meet these minimum requirements, forcing one to get out of the narrow confines of one's place of employment and to get fresh viewpoints. Most conscientious workers, aware that professional development is their personal responsibility, go far beyond the usual minimum requirements in keeping abreast of new developments in the field.

Regular reading of professional journals and new books, attendance at conventions and workshops, and taking additional courses are some ways to keep up. Those who feel they have nothing else to learn once they have qualified for an initial credential are a danger to the profession and to patients. One could ask, "When is the last time I read a research paper or attended a conference *not* as a requirement for renewal of credentials?" (See NIAAA 1991, *Linking Alcoholism Treatment Research with Clinical Practice*.)

Since going beyond one's competence is forbidden by all ethical codes, we must constantly stay alert to learn more about our limitations and to be able to recognize when it is in the best interest of the patients to release them or refer them elsewhere. Limitations may stem from a lack of training or experience, unfamiliarity with the area in which the problem falls, the difficulty or complexity of the case, or interpersonal problems between patient and counselor. Problem solving in any of these areas may be aided by continuing education, and having a clinical supervisor can prevent serious problems (Powell 1988).

CHAPTER THREE

RIGHTS OF PATIENTS

THE MYTH OF CHOICE

Another major and unique problem in the field of counseling chemically dependent people is the status of the patient. Most treatment facilities will maintain that their patients are there voluntarily and have given informed consent to both treatment and release of information. This is often nonsense. It may be true that a patient has not been legally committed to treatment, that the doorknob turns from the inside, and that anyone can leave at any time. It may be equally true that if the patient does leave, he or she may lose a job, a professional license, or the custody of his or her children. Sometimes a jail sentence will result.

Unlike the committed mental patient with a host of safeguards and legal regulations, the alcoholic or other user is not supplied with legal counsel and an outside physician advocate, nor does the institution have to show that meaningful treatment is being provided. While some states can and do commit patients for addictive illness, many do not. Even in states where this is legally possible, most patients are still treated in what are called "voluntary settings." People are forced into treatment in a variety of ways. Very few arrive without some outside pressure. Patients may sign away confidentiality safeguards under duress or while still so toxic that they are unable to appreciate the consequences.

We live in a society that tries to solve many social problems by passing increasingly strict laws, building more jail cells, and increasing the severity of penalties. Mandatory sentencing is stylish, and there is an increasing outcry to get impaired drivers off the road. Once an impaired driver has been caught, something more must be done. If this is not just careless misbehavior and the real problem is alcohol or other drugs, doesn't it make sense to mandate treatment as an alternative to, or in addition to, punishment? Who then decides on the treatment? Where and by whom will it be given? What is the role of the state in deciding who needs treatment, what treatment is, who will give it, and who will make money from doing so? One hopes that the patient will be the one who benefits, but politics play a big part in the decision.

Individuals with drug dependency problems are still not seen by the public as people whose rights must be defended. Not every state-licensed treatment agency does a good job of caring for its patients, and some agencies actually do harm. This is a situation that may well get worse before it improves.

Can we do without coercion? Probably not, unless we are willing to stand by and watch a great many people die as in the past. Alcoholism and other chemical dependencies are characterized by denial and self-delusion. Initially, patients may be no more capable of making well-reasoned and informed judgments in their own behalf than small children. For a time, particularly early in treatment, the responsible therapist must accept that the patient is not able to make good decisions and that a little bit of creative coercion and outside pressure is not entirely bad. But how long does this situation last? How valid is that signed consent for release of information when it is obtained under duress? What does the demand to cooperate with treatment or lose a job or license really entail? Since real mental impairment follows the heavy use of alcohol or other drugs, and since the treatment facility may have given the patient even more drugs that affect judgment (in detox, for example), how valid is a written consent?

MEETING PATIENTS' INDIVIDUAL NEEDS

Counselors, other treatment professionals, and law enforcement agencies are in a position of tremendous power. This is an unavoidable and probably acceptable situation if what is being done is in the patient's best interest. When the decision makers are ignorant, incompetent, or self-serving, the risks are obvious. Potential conflicts of interest abound. Although the true situation may be disguised on paper, the person who forces a colleague into treatment may be the very one who runs the treatment program the patient is attending. Sometimes the patient has no choice as to where to go or what kind of treatment to expect. This is clearly dangerous. If people are forced to accept unwanted treatment for their own good, they should experience as little deprivation of freedom as possible. The person choosing the treatment facility should have no opportunity to profit from it in any way, including by financial gain, by an increase in personal status, or by trading favors. There should be no conflict of interest, overt or concealed, real or apparent.

One way this problem has been approached, if never perfectly solved, follows a time-honored medical tradition. Once a problem has been defined and the decision made to refer a person for treatment, he or she should be offered a choice of acceptable treatment facilities, if possible. This should be a free choice situation, not a listing of several alternates with a covert message that if the referent's preference is ignored someone will be angry or retaliate.

It is tempting for an employer or professional society to enter into a contractual arrangement with a single treatment facility. Staff can learn to know each other and work together smoothly, cost arrangements can be adjusted to reflect a large volume of referrals, and beds can be made available when they might otherwise be hard to obtain. It all seems efficient, simple—and tempting.

A worrisome development is the entry of employers and unions into the business of providing treatment for their own employees. Faced with soaring insurance costs and often located in communities that failed to provide outpatient treatment services, both groups have begun to set up their own programs. They are less expensive than residential care and will probably demonstrate good treatment outcome results, since a lack of financial incentives have, in the past, resulted in much unnecessary residential treatment.

The problem is that not only are employers now forcing patients into unwanted treatment, but diagnosis and treatment are both being decided on by fellow employees. This can result in not only the risk of suboptimal treatment based on budget considerations but also possible gossip and unfairness in treatment requirements and evaluations, as everyone works for the same employer and is subject to the same in-house jealousies and politics. The risks are obvious; the legal and ethical implications may be less so (see Nye and Kaiser 1990).

Treatment for chemical dependency needs to be individualized as for any other illness. No particular treatment facility is the best place for every patient. Different facilities have different strengths and weaknesses. Some are particularly good for women, some for older people, some for youngsters. Some are racist. Some offer excellent programs for family members. Some offer good medical or psychiatric care in addition to their basic treatment program. Some specialize in pain management. Some are short term while others offer extended stay. The list of possible differences is very long.

Not only do facilities differ, but most show changes in the quality of care they give at different times. Treatment often reflects the personality and convictions of one or more highly individualistic leaders. When staff members change or when they go through periods of not relating well to one another, patient care may suffer. Resources need to be checked intermittently to be sure that the quality of care at any given treatment facility is acceptable. Whenever most of the referrals from a particular employer or organization are sent to the same program for treatment, the situation should be carefully scrutinized. It is unlikely that treatment is being tailored to the needs of each individual patient, and there is a risk that a bargain may have been struck between the referral source and treatment agency.

EVALUATION OF TREATMENT SUCCESS

Until recently, health care providers were rarely asked to justify treatment costs or to demonstrate their efficacy. To be ill and in pain was considered enough to establish a person's right to treatment. Even if the effort to help proved inadequate, there was agreement that it should be made. Alcohol or other drug problems, however, were regarded differently. Government policymakers and insurance carriers have constantly demanded objective research to prove that treating addiction is both successful and cost-effective. Employee assistance programs are constantly asked to point out savings in absenteeism, accidents, and property damage when chemical dependency is treated, while the obese person's diabetes and the heavy smoker's chronic bronchitis, emphysema, and circulatory problems are covered by insurance and treated without question. Not only are employees expected to demonstrate to employers that chemical dependency treatment is deserved, but the treatment agency is also expected to prove to employers and insurance carriers that their treatment works.

There are good reasons to track and justify treatment results. On the whole, alcoholism and addiction treatment results are respectable and encouraging. In an age of increasing worry about the cost of health care and the inevitable need for rationing, it is increasingly important to have research data in hand and to have experience in collecting it. However, we are too often presented with "research" that is little more than a treatment agency's bragging about its program's success, obviously less convincing than evaluation by a disinterested and objective outsider. Sometimes the results are clear, accurate, and useful, but they may also be sloppy, misleading, and invented. If we are to retain credibility and share useful information with one another about what works for patients and what does not, we need to insist on quality data and well-defined goals. We also need to distinguish fact from philosophy.

For example, there is an ongoing quarrel over the efficacy of methadone maintenance programs for heroin addicts. Some people, especially those in the chemical dependency field, argue that the primary treatment goal must be a drug-free lifestyle. Others familiar with the street scene argue that while abstinence may be the ideal, indefinite methadone maintenance is the lesser of two evils when the amount of violent crime perpetrated by actively using heroin addicts is examined.

It is also worth mentioning that only a relatively small group of conditions have ever been treated with painful electric shock, inappropriate lobotomy procedures, and other punitive methods. These include homosexuality, child molestation (where even castration has been proposed), and chemical dependency. Stigma has been and is still a major problem. When society is particularly outraged and judgmental about certain groups or behaviors, we must be alert to the difference between treatment and punishment under the guise of treatment.

For many of the issues raised in this book, there are no easy answers. But we can insist on strict accountability, honest self-appraisal, and accurate reporting of treatment goals and results rather than rhetoric and opinion. The scandal is not that there are different approaches to measuring success, but that there hasn't been enough objective, outside, long-term evaluation of treatment methods. We may have a tendency to overlook facts that do not reinforce our preconceived, emotionally derived opinions.

We would also do well not to exaggerate the number of alcoholic and other drug-dependent people in society. We need not argue that we are always in a new crisis or suffering a new epidemic, any more than we need pretend that one treatment method has all the answers for every patient. The truth about drug problems in our society is serious enough; it scarcely needs to be inflated. The misery caused by alcohol and other drugs is more than enough to keep us all busy for a long time to come.

CONFIDENTIALITY

The ethics of professional confidentiality bring up a host of complicated issues. The basic principle is that private information divulged by patients in the course of treatment may never be used or repeated in any way that can be identified with the patient. This allows for research and for generalized statements, providing they do not stigmatize all the clients of a given facility. Note that we say "private information," because sometimes the counselor may also know the facts from another source, even a public one. Professionals must not reveal any information, including the fact that a particular person is a patient in a treatment facility, without first obtaining written consent while the patient is rational and drug free. If such consent is not obtained, professionals may not share private information, not even with a trusted colleague or spouse. This is true even if the counselor sincerely believes that the patient would be helped by the disclosure.

Privileged communication is a legal term, referring to the practice of excusing many professionals, such as physicians, nurses, clergy, psychologists, and others, from being compelled to testify in court. States vary as to which professionals are included. Addiction counselors, unless they happen to also belong to a profession named in the statute, usually must testify under subpoena (a summons to appear in court). In some states these legal exclusions also apply to someone whom the patient reasonably believes to be a licensed professional, which could include a counselor. The privilege can be claimed or waived only by the client or patient. Furthermore, even when the patient has waived the legal right, the professional may still have an ethical obligation to protect the patient's best interests.

Regardless of legal privilege, professionals are ethically obliged to respect the confidentiality of the patient, so an implied contract or promise always exists. But it is never absolute—exceptions can occur. We may be obliged to violate confidentiality by informing an intended victim or the police when there is clear and imminent danger of serious harm to our patient or another person. Note that the danger must be clear, not vague, and imminent, not merely possible. And it must be of serious harm, not minor or merely inconvenient.

Professional consultation in difficult cases is allowed, but the consultant is equally bound to confidentiality. Both ethics and federal law both provide for the right of a counselor to consult an attorney, or a doctor for a medical emergency, but neither provides for a warrant that allows drug enforcement officers to hunt suspected addicts. Some statutes except homicide and malpractice cases as instances where disclosure of confidential information is allowed. Another exception is in cases where the patient's purpose in disclosing information was to seek advice in the furtherance of a crime or fraud. Staff policy manuals should indicate these exceptions, and the patient should be informed.

There are a host of other confidentiality concerns. Clerical staff must be instructed about the confidentiality of records and correspondence. Volunteers must not be given access to files, and they must be warned that even the names of people who are admitted is private information. A supervisor may not ask a counselor what was said at an A.A. meeting. Group therapy leaders must spell out the explicit obligation of confidentiality to all group members, including therapists (Gazda 1978). Visitors, too, may present a problem if a staff member wants to invite someone to stay for a meal. Some are people unable to resist gossiping about who they see.

The United States government has issued strict detailed regulations on confidentiality of chemical dependency treatment records ("Confidentiality" 1975, 1982). These rules are more strict than those that cover other health care providers. For instance, while the presence of a particular person as a patient in a general hospital may be public knowledge, the diagnosis and other details remain confidential.

But the very fact that a person is a patient in a treatment facility for chemical dependency is itself a diagnosis, so it cannot be revealed without express written consent. Nor can it be denied, however, as this could suggest an individual had been a patient, but has since left the facility. One can only answer, "Federal law forbids me to say anything." Moreover, the usual signed consent for disclosure of information to other agencies or professionals will not suffice; it must specify to whom the disclosure will be made and set a time limit. Even the disclosure of this authorized information to another agency without explicit consent is forbidden. Federal rules allow the courts to authorize disclosure of confidential information, but this only removes the prohibition and does not require disclosure.

Sometimes a third-party payer insists on seeing records in order to prove that medical care is necessary and hence reimbursable. This is an especially difficult situation. An ethically sound rule seems to be to release only the bare minimum of information necessary to get our patients their insurance coverage, without revealing any private details that would damage the patient's reputation or jeopardize further employment. Information released for the purposes of third-party payment should be sent only to the medical director of the carrier or that director's department and not routed through the employer, the union, the patient, or the patient's family. In addition, all released information should be stamped "Confidential: Federal Law Prohibits Further Disclosure." (See Blume 1977, 1987.)

Careful record keeping is necessary to protect the rights of patients and colleagues. Under no circumstances should a chart be doctored when it is subpoenaed.

CONFIDENTIALITY AND CHILD-ABUSE ISSUES

Problems involving conflict of laws are always difficult. Such was the situation when state laws requiring the report of child abuse conflicted with the federal law that even the presence of the patient in a treatment facility is confidential (NIAAA 1979). Some ethicians argued that equity places the right of a child not to be abused above the right of an abuser not to be identified as chemically dependent. Others maintained that confidentiality should take precedence, lest parents with alcohol or other drug problems be deterred from entering treatment for fear of losing their children (Lewis 1983, King 1983).

Congress resolved the legal conflict by passing public law 99-401 in August 1986. It amends federal law (42 U.S. Code ss290dd-3 and ee-3) by adding the sentence "The prohibitions of this section do not apply to the reporting under state law of incidents of suspected child abuse or neglect to the appropriate state authorities." The new statute applies only to initial reports of child abuse or neglect and not to requests for additional information or records. According to Rep. Don Edwards, Chair of the Judiciary Subcommittee on Civil and Constitutional Rights, it does not affect the subsection requiring a court order before records may be used to initiate or substantiate any criminal charges, or to conduct any investigation of a patient.

Also, the restriction on reporting is removed only when there is actual danger or harm to the child; reporting merely because a parent has a problem with alcohol or other drugs is not permitted. The statute thus maintains maximum possible concern for confidentiality even in cases involving suspected child abuse. Procedure manuals must reflect this balance and should provide for notifying patients of this exception to their expected confidentiality rights.

Legality aside, some ethical problems remain. Requiring that all chemically dependent parents be reported would jeopardize many treatment programs as word spread through the community that entering treatment would lead directly to a child abuse investigation. Moreover, it would clog the child protection system and impede efforts to combat actual child abuse. When attempts are made to jail pregnant addicts in an attempt to protect the fetus, some women avoid all health care providers until the actual time of birth. Some even resort to abortion rather than face jail. Some women have been prosecuted after delivery and their infants taken from them on the charge of delivering drugs to a minor through the umbilical cord (e.g., *Jackson v. Florida*).

In child-abuse cases our natural concern for the child may override our awareness of the rights of the accused. As a result, the presumption that one is innocent until proven guilty can easily yield to a presumption of guilt by mere accusation (Gardner 1991). This is further complicated by a growing trend of therapists suggesting "repressed" memories of child abuse through regression therapy, sometimes using guided imagery, hypnosis, or massage—all of which heighten suggestibility. The unreliability of some of these supposed "memories" is confirmed by the fifty cases of retraction reported by Berkeley psychologist Dr. Margaret Singer, and by the research of Dr. Elizabeth Loftus, a University of Washington professor of psychology and law who is an expert on memory in testimony. Ethics and sound clinical practice both seem to support using only the patient's own words in therapy, not adding to or embellishing his or her version of the incident.

MANDATORY DRUG TESTING

It may be useful to put the issue of mandatory drug testing in historical perspective. Prior to the decriminalization efforts of the early 1970s, alcoholism and other drug dependencies were regarded as crimes, and jails were seen as a better place for drug-dependent people than treatment centers. Finally we learned that putting people who were ill in cages didn't cure alcoholism or other drug dependencies any more than it cured other diseases.

In the early 1980s the pendulum swung again toward a massive law-and-order initiative. MADD (Mothers Against Drunk Driving), RID (Remove Intoxicated Drivers), SADD (Students Against Driving Drunk), and other citizen groups organized around the problem of drunk driving and insisted that punishment and treatment each had a place and that limits had to be set. Parents and retailers who provided alcohol to juveniles or people who are obviously intoxicated were held responsible along with the impaired driver. Parent groups increasingly espoused tough love, often emphasizing the first of those two words.

Into this climate came reports of the government's failure to stem the use of heroin, marijuana, and cocaine, and headlines shouted about the crack epidemic. Prior to the 1984 election, the Republican and Democratic parties vied to see which could take the hardest stance on drugs, and candidates were publicly challenging each other to take urine tests. Massive amounts of money were spent on discovering drug users, but very little was allocated for research or treatment. Some was earmarked for prevention, but much more went for interdiction attempts or other law enforcement. Funding was provided for more jail cells, more prosecutors, more border guards, more aircraft at the borders, and more pressure on Latin American countries whose economies are heavily dependent on the export of drugs to the United States.

Along with all of this came an increasing demand for urine tests to reveal illicit drug use. Drug and AIDS testing became routine in the military. A number of employers began testing current and new employees. Wholesale testing of federal employees was urged, and policymakers backed off only when employees fought back, leaving the decision of who should be tested to individual departments. The subject of drug testing became hotly debated in the courts.

What does this have to do with ethics? The argument is raised that if we have nothing to hide, why should we object to being tested? The Florida Medical Association expressed its willingness to have member physicians tested. Is this our business? Must we professionals take a position on any of this and, if so, how?

In the authors' opinion, we should. If the "nothing to hide" argument were valid, then we shouldn't object to having someone read our mail, browse through our personal medical records, or peek into our bedrooms. The preservation of the Bill of Rights and the privacy of every individual is worth more than the risk of failing to catch an individual who drinks or uses other drugs. These are not simple choices and must be carefully weighed, not made on impulse.

Ingenious ways of beating the urine test are multiplying and clean urine is selling well where tests are required. There is only one way to collect a urine specimen and be certain of whose it is; it is embarrassing for all concerned but essential if we are to bother with urine testing at all. What does this do to the trust relationship that should be building between patient and counselor when the counselor is involved in this process?

There are many problems with the testing mechanism itself as well. For instance, many testing programs ignore the most commonly used drug in America: alcohol. Furthermore, available tests can be expensive or inaccurate, sometimes both. Any positive results need to be confirmed using another type of test to ensure accuracy, and the chain of custody of the sample must be protected to prevent substitution. Results are further complicated because most tests indicate only use, not addiction. Clinical evaluation of the employee by an experienced addiction worker is still necessary, since the distinctions between use, abuse, and addiction require more expertise than is possessed by most who will see the test results.

There is also little assurance that use of the test results, even when accurate, will be limited to their stated purpose. Affordable treatment remains scarce and there is little to prevent employers from using test results to get rid of certain employees while keeping others. Employers should not terminate anyone until he or she has had an appropriate evaluation for addictive disorder and the opportunity to participate in a rehabilitation program.

What if the test is also used to detect pregnancy? What if a barbiturate is detected in the urine of an epileptic who needs it for a legitimate medical propose but who may be fired or lose a promotion if the reason for its use becomes known? The National Council on

Alcoholism and Drug Dependence (NCADD) issued a policy statement on mandatory testing in 1993 which contains many cautions and limitations, concluding that a good employee assistance program (EAP) is usually preferable.

Again, we need to think this through and take appropriate actions. This may include speaking out against random testing (as opposed to testing when there is evidence of impairment and a demonstrable effect on job performance), but may also include a personal refusal to be tested. If refuseniks are few in number and the rest of us meekly go along, it will be easy to claim that a person must be guilty because of refusal. If enough of us who object are clearly unlikely to be using, that claim will be less plausible. The choice here is not limited to protecting privacy versus letting potentially dangerous employees pilot airplanes or operate heavy machinery. There are a variety of ways to monitor competence that do not require invasive medical tests.

Even when we are secure in knowing our own aims, values, and ideals, the ways in which they are applied remain endlessly varied. Never easy, never static, the striving for "progress, not perfection" doesn't end. It can lead to some of the most painful choices we have to make and some of the most satisfying.

AIDS

A person caught in the web of alcoholism or another addiction will often make thoughtless remarks, drive while impaired, get into domestic squabbles if not actual violence, and participate in a variety of sexual activities that are impulsive, unplanned, often unwanted, and sometimes dangerous. One woman summed up a lot of personal history by saying that one of the rewards of abstinence was waking in the morning without having to ask, "Who are you and where are we?"

We live in the age of AIDS, a disease profoundly changing our society. AIDS is caused by HIV, the human immunodeficiency virus, not a lifestyle. The spread of AIDS and our survival depend on what we do. Unfortunately, its first victims in the United States were the very people who are favorite targets of the bigots—gay men, prostitutes, intravenous drug users, and Haitians. There were others as well, but their numbers are much fewer: people with hemophilia, those who had received HIV-contaminated blood transfusions, infants born to mothers who were carrying the virus during pregnancy, and heterosexuals.

Much of the public managed to persuade itself that HIV infection and AIDS would not spread into the heterosexual community. Concern for those dying of AIDS was minimal. Some even sat in judgment on its victims, and some (a physician among them) said this was God's punishment for their sexual orientation or their drug use.

Changes have occurred. We know HIV infection is difficult to catch except through sexual contact, the use of needles contaminated with blood, or the transfusion of blood products. One does not get it from sharing a table, a toilet seat, or a swimming pool. It is not spread by a group hug or a kiss on the cheek. Parents do more for their children's health and safety by using seat belts properly or refraining from smoking around their children than by becoming hysterical over whether or not a youngster with AIDS is in the same elementary school. (See the excellent statement by former U.S. Surgeon General, C. Everett Koop 1986.)

Another major change is the knowledge that HIV infection and AIDS have now spread into the heterosexual community. HIV has arrived in every state and in every social class. The number of people who have the virus but who are not members of high-risk groups grows steadily, particularly among young people. This will continue. The group now accounting for most of the new cases are addicts and their sexual partners, not homosexuals. Most of us who treat chemically dependent people are already treating people who have been infected with HIV. Some of us will discover that we too have been infected, although not by our patients. Some appear entirely well and may remain that way while still carrying the virus and being capable of infecting others. A few of our patients have AIDS itself. There are many stages in between.

When there is a disaster, most people feel free to save themselves first, but traditionally certain professionals have been expected to stay and help others. These include doctors, nurses, clergy, ship captains, firefighters, police, and the military. Addiction counselors are still too new a profession to have much guiding tradition. The very first people treating people with AIDS demonstrated great courage. They cared for these patients before it was clear that the disease wasn't contagious through casual contact.

While other diseases, such as cancer or emphysema, present complications in the treatment setting, AIDS presents a special challenge more because of our feelings about it than the problems it presents. We have to deal with the irrational fears of both patients and colleagues. Patients have been abruptly discharged from treatment because administrators feared that if their presence were known, other patients would leave or stay away, the census might drop, and money would be lost. This persists, even though patients with HIV or AIDS are not dangerous to others. We know now that usually there is a period of ten years or more between the time a person is infected with HIV and becomes ill with AIDS itself. These are potentially good years of productive, sober, drug-free living when a person can benefit from treatment.

If someone does have HIV or AIDS, we are faced with the same situation we face with many cancer patients: a patient whose comfort and physical condition can be improved, who will probably go through periods of seeming recovery, but whose time remains limited. Any dying person brings us face-to-face with our own mortality and limitations. Our time for dying will come. We are powerless to cure, we can only delay. To make it worse, AIDS patients are often young, not elderly. Perhaps the knowledge that there will be an end to life is one of the major differences between ourselves and other animals, but it is not easy knowledge to fully accept. How tempting to rationalize that since a patient's days are numbered, we could better use our time and energy on others. It is much harder to admit we're uneasy, sometimes at a loss for words, and searching for an excuse to run away rather than stand beside the patient and face together what's coming, and do it without the use of drugs.

When the fear of contagion has been laid to rest and the reality of a possible premature death is understood, there may remain another problem. If the patient is gay, some counselors who have not worked through their homophobia may shun the patient. Homosexuality isn't contagious either. Men or women secure in their sexual identity have nothing to fear and no need to attack. If working with a gay man or a lesbian is uncomfortable for a counselor, one of two roads can be followed: either work out the feelings, or acknowledge the limitation and let someone else work with that person (Finnegan and McNally 1987, Gosselin and Nice 1987). It's difficult enough to have AIDS, to be gay or lesbian in the present social climate, or to admit to being an alcoholic or an addict. The last thing a patient needs is to be counseled by someone who disapproves of who that patient is. If we can't really accept and love, let's get out of the way and make room for those who can.

CHAPTER FOUR

EXPLOITATION

The chemically dependent patient is vulnerable to exploitation in a variety of ways. In early recovery the patient experiences confusion and impaired judgment directly resulting from alcohol or other drug use. Later, if all goes well, there may be a honeymoon period of enormous relief, as understanding and optimism begin to replace the fear and misery of active addiction. Gratitude toward treatment staff naturally follows, and the therapist may be perceived as an all-knowing and trustworthy guru. This is a time when the patient is vulnerable to the imposition of the goals and values of others and needs protection against impulsive and superficially considered actions.

FINANCIAL CONTACTS WITH PATIENTS

The medical world has long recognized that its major benefactors tend to come from those who have benefited from treatment. A person who is fresh from a serious operation and is pleased with the outcome cannot help but be interested in the hospital and the people who have made the miracle. Who better to solicit for money for the new surgical wing? If the request is not made fairly promptly, the risk is that the patient will simply go on with life, forget the virtues of the staff, the excellence of the treatment, and focus on other things.

The same process applies to chemical dependency, but there are differences. Those who undergo surgery are soon thereafter presumed to be in control of their mental processes, and although impressed by and grateful to the surgeon, they are not as likely to be ensnarled in the strong but unrecognized bonds of transference. Addicts have frequently been through tumultuous emotional experiences and may not be capable of thinking straight for some time—six months? a year? two years? The likeliest donors to treatment centers are former patients and their families. They know the kind of work that is done there and have experienced its benefits, but we must proceed with caution and wait until former patients are fully able to make important financial decisions and appreciate the consequences. We must allow them more time than for other patients before they can ethically be solicited for donations. Unlike those in other types of hospitals, many chemical dependency patients will return for aftercare, alumni activities, and Twelve Step programs. They need not be lost when they leave residential treatment, and there is no reason to pester them for donations early in recovery.

PUBLICITY

Exploitation can be for social as well as financial gain. When a treatment facility has a celebrity as a patient, someone may decide to let the news leak out, thus gaining widespread publicity for the institution. If the facility limits its patients to people with alcohol or other drug problems, someone's presence there as a patient makes public the diagnosis. In spite of recent gains in public acceptance of people seeking recovery, such a diagnosis continues to carry a degree of stigma. Sometimes patients are blackmailed into believing it a personal duty to diminish this stigma by permitting the media to reveal that they are still in or have been freshly discharged from a particular treatment facility, and to imply that others may also recover after treatment there. While one can certainly make a case for coming out of the closet in a variety of situations, this is not a decision that should be made impulsively or without consideration of long-range effects on other family members, colleagues, and career.

There is little problem with people who, two or three years after treatment, decide the time is right and who wish to make this experience public. But when someone at the treatment center goes on camera with a patient still in treatment or urges that person to speak for the local alcoholism council after only three months of sobriety, this can be exploitative and brings little real glory to the institution that encourages it. The ethics of posing such a request should be carefully weighed, even if the person involved agrees eagerly to do it. How sound is the judgment of the newly recovered person? And what exactly, and for whose benefit, is all the haste? A.A. and other Twelve Step group members may ponder for months over when and how to break anonymity and are careful to let each member decide this matter according to individual circumstance. Very few regret having waited; many more wish they had been less hasty.

SOCIAL CONTACTS WITH PATIENTS

Most difficult of all is the question of social contact between counselor and patient when the concerns are not the more clear-cut cash-register or "principles above personalities" issues discussed above. Regardless of legal definitions of sexual harassment or court rulings, there is an ethical demand that we take a hard look at the psychological harm done to patients when professional trust is violated. Whether there is mutual consent or even seduction by the patient, the therapist is still fully responsible for what happens. State accrediting boards and associations need to get tough on offenders and not be swayed by the good-old-boy approach of a few decades ago. While taking care to protect the rights of the accused, and holding one innocent until proven guilty in the best of American legal tradition, investigations of complaints need to be prompt and thorough. And professionals at all levels must be willing to blow the whistle on a colleague, putting professional integrity above personal friendship, cowardice, or indifference.

The extremes are fairly easy to recognize. Should a counselor enter into a dating or sexual relationship with a patient in treatment? The ethical codes of all helping professions forbid this. Is such a relationship all right two weeks after treatment has ended? No. Well, what about six months? a year? two years? ever? Is the transference phenomenon one that will disappear after a certain length of time, or does it remain forever? Can the helper/helpee relationship be neutralized by time and insight so that the counselor is perceived as just one more person and not expected to be parent, caretaker, and expert?

Can the counselor, in turn, stop expecting continuing gratitude and adoration from the former patient, whom the counselor may see as his or her own creation rather than just as a lover? And why is a former patient the only one with the special magic to catch the counselor's heart? What really is happening? Counselors need to be aware of the dynamics of transference and countertransference and of the need to help patients free themselves, as opposed to unconsciously fostering a dependence that may be flattering to the counselor but which stunts the patient's growth. Counselors must be trained in how to handle separation anxiety and how to terminate relationships gracefully. This is a problem in all the helping professions, even among psychiatrists, who are generally trained to recognize and resolve countertransference issues (Rutter 1989, Peterson 1992, Schoener et al. 1989, Gartrell et al. 1986).

The American Psychiatric Association struggled between two ethical positions: to recommend a waiting period of perhaps two years of no contact or to forbid absolutely all romantic entanglements whatsoever between therapist and former patient. They finally decided to recommend no sexual relationship, regardless of time—no phone calls, no Christmas cards, nothing—a difficult but wise decision with which the authors concur, after some initial reluctance of appearing too rigid on the issue. Experience shows that such relationships are rarely if ever healthy.

One reason why social and sexual contacts with former patients are more complex in the addiction field than those faced by most mental health professionals lies in the nature of the illness itself. Mutual-help groups, where socializing may occur and where there is often no facilitator, may compound the problem further. After a variable period of time, most addicts who remain abstinent from alcohol or other drugs do recover. Although their behavior during active addiction may have been outrageous, with time they can become well. Addiction counselors are well aware of this. They believe in full recovery and communicate this basic belief to their patients because they know it is true. A person desperately ill and incapable of good reality testing today may in two or three years be better than normal.

There is little temptation for most psychotherapists to involve their social lives with their more seriously ill present and former patients, some of whom are expected, rightly or wrongly, to remain ill. Psychotherapists who did so would be regarded with dismay by their colleagues, and their own mental health would be questioned. Counselors in chemical dependency work can expect to find many of their former patients well, happy, productive, and attractive in many ways, and unlike psychotherapists, they can expect to see former patients in shared support-group settings in the future. These former patients will be regarded as healthy and socially acceptable by colleagues as well. Most mental health workers, on the other hand, are quite unlikely to end up as equal members of a therapy group with patients they have had in treatment.

A.A. RELATIONSHIPS WITH PATIENTS
The world of A.A. and similar support groups can also present some relationship puzzles. Some treatment facilities have actually required A.A. members on their staffs to sponsor their own patients, a risky merging of two quite different roles that are, at best, not easy to keep separate. The A.A., N.A., and Al-Anon communities are

fairly limited in size. Even in large cities, counselors often find themselves sharing an A.A. group with former or present patients, and have to decide how self-revealing they can be in this situation. Since abstinence, even survival itself, may depend on regular use of the group, the presence of the patient may cause problems. The counselor needs to insist on whatever is necessary to ensure his or her own sobriety, which may mean being quite firm with patients who innocently feel that the patterns of the treatment setting are to be continued in the A.A. world. (See Gregson and Summers 1992.)

In cities it is often feasible for staff and patients to find separate groups. In small towns this may be impossible. When an entire group may consist of only twenty members, and when most of the group habitually goes to a post-meeting coffee klatch together, does the counselor also go along and socialize with former patients or march off alone into the night? Today's patient in treatment becomes tomorrow's peer at A.A. Is there a solution or a right way to behave? No one has provided an answer that works for everyone.

There is general agreement that counselors must think through the roles of A.A. and of treatment, avoid confusing A.A. with their professional and social life, and then be cautious. It helps to ask others for input on what the implications of different courses of action may be. One thoughtful person suggested that while a certain amount of A.A. contact with patients was inevitable, most of the traps could be avoided by two measures: One is to make no scheduled appointments with former patients, although creating awkward and artificial measures to avoid casual contact is impractical. The other is to avoid situations where one might be alone with former patients, particularly those of the opposite sex.

There are other sets of ground rules. A.A. *Guidelines: For Members Employed in the Alcoholism Field* (Alcoholics Anonymous 1993) is a gold mine of common sense and experience, a main theme being that there is a great difference between functioning as a chemical dependency professional and as an A.A. member and that it is important to recognize which hat one is wearing.

SHOULD ALCOHOLICS DRINK?

A controversial issue is the attempt by some behavioral scientists to condition recovered alcoholics to drink socially or in moderation. While recognizing the value of research and the freedom to pursue scientific knowledge, the ethician must raise other considerations as well. Given the present state of our knowledge, is it ethical to risk continued exposure to a life-threatening drug? The consensus in the alcoholism field is that the evidence does not warrant it and that abstinence is the only legitimate treatment goal.

Even if some recovered alcoholics might continue to drink without major adverse consequences, their numbers are few and they cannot be identified in advance. Research may continue with those whose alcoholism remains in doubt, those for whom all other forms of treatment have failed, and those who really do reject abstinence as a treatment goal. Perhaps this is the only way some people can learn for themselves what they have been unable to learn from others: that for almost all, this approach will eventually fail. It dispels the rationalization that they could drink moderately "if they really tried" when they fail even with all this scientific help. We need to be sure that the refusal to abstain is the decision of the patient, not the preference of the therapist who has promoted it. This issue is not to be confused with the work of Marlatt and others on behavior modification techniques aimed at relapse prevention rather than at successful drinking for alcoholics.

Less clear is the question of what ethical obligations we have toward informing those at high risk of alcoholism, such as children of alcoholic parents, and what ethical restraints these people should impose on their own drinking behavior.

CHAPTER FIVE

ECONOMICS, FUNDS, AND FICTIONS

INSURANCE

Alcoholism is among the most common serious illnesses in the United States—the most common being heart disease. If we combine alcoholism with the other chemical dependencies, the numbers are even greater. It seems logical that the most common ailments would routinely be given a proportionate amount of attention in health care teaching and that hospitals and health insurers would have worked out the most efficient, reasonable, and effective ways of dealing with them by now. This, however, has not been the case.

A legacy of the Prohibition era is the moralistic posture that these are self-inflicted illnesses and symptoms of weakness—if not outright badness. Seen as a sin or social problem then, chemical dependency seems not to be the legitimate responsibility of the health care system. The use of street drugs carries with it the additional tarnish of illegality, and the less visible problem of prescription drugs, enormous though it is, has failed to arouse much public interest or concern.

As recently as the 1960s it was not unusual to find hospital rules spelling out that alcoholics were not to be admitted, and the physician who openly insisted on doing so risked losing hospital privileges. When laws changed and hospitals were ordered not to discriminate against alcoholics, insurance coverage lagged far behind. Of course alcoholics got admitted anyway. Not only were there comfortable drying-out spas for the wealthy, but hospitals, too, found room for the affluent, the interesting, and the privileged chemically dependent. Most could and did pay their own way since little insurance coverage was available. Treatment was often limited to brief periods of detoxification.

DIAGNOSTIC SUBTERFUGE

Over the years and into the 1970s, patients were frequently admitted, as they always had been, not with a primary diagnosis of alcoholism or other addiction, but under another label that would be both socially acceptable and, more to the point, reimbursable by health insurance. In many cases there was more than one honest choice of diagnosis. If the patient suffered from cirrhosis of the liver, gastro-enteritis, a bleeding problem, severe anxiety, organic brain syndrome, or depression, any of these could be presented as the primary problem and treatment costs were then paid. Other patients showed fewer physical problems, and the physician often had to exaggerate complications to guarantee payment. In other cases, these complications had to be invented. What to call the problem varied with the hospital or type of facility eligible for reimbursement.

If this system worked and ways were found to cover both the patient's and the hospital's expenses without unreasonably penalizing someone who had contracted an unpopular illness, why was this so bad?

There are several reasons. Such a system discourages the design of specialized services for chemically dependent patients because it is hard to set aside beds for a condition that does not officially exist. When one considers the poor insurance coverage for alcoholism today, the situation is even more frustrating, since alcoholism treatment has become more competent and more effective.

Inappropriate insurance patterns also create an unfortunate doctor-patient relationship. Either the physician tells the truth and the insurance company denies coverage, or the doctor conceals the truth and colludes in defrauding the insurance system. Kind and lofty though the motives may be, the resulting behavior is not honest.

When a physician lies about a diagnosis, be it to guarantee payment, spare the patient's reputation, or permit hospital admission in the first place, something else happens. The physician is now established as a liar. It is important that patients be able to believe their therapists, particularly when what they are asked to believe contains a great deal that they would prefer not to hear. After a dishonest beginning, how does the therapist go on to convince the evasive, denying, and mistrustful alcoholic of the need for candor and openness, and explain the honesty part of Twelve Step programs?

Many people agree that regulations are too often unreasonable and rules don't make sense. Some people feel that working the system in whatever way is necessary to help a patient might be a justifiable form of civil disobedience. The goal is to heal the sick and make people well. But people who feel the need for accurate information object. They point out that if all the people who die of alcoholism are reported as having died of heart disease instead, the true impact of chemical dependency has been hidden. We can't protect the memory of the dead by concealing the facts and then bemoan our lack of data. Hiding both treatment and death behind inaccurate diagnoses deprives us of statistical evidence that might help demonstrate a need for policy changes. Without such evidence, the task of developing more rational systems is slowed.

ENTER THE FAMILY

Treatment has increasingly become reimbursable without the subterfuge deplored above, but many problems remain. As the needs of the family are recognized and as more professionals become convinced that family programs play an important part in both the patient's and the family's recovery, many programs have been designed. Residential programs offer an intense short-term experience of less than a week consisting of basic education and some therapy. Family members live together in a controlled setting, which can help them learn from each other and free them from the distractions of home and job. Family programs offer space and a little time for significant others to examine the behaviors they've developed in response to living in the insane ambiance of active addiction.

Some insurance companies still have reservations about treating seriously ill addicts specifically for addiction rather than for its late physical manifestations or simple detoxification. How then are they to regard a demand that treatment also be provided to the family member who has the illness once removed? If a man married an alcoholic just last week is he then in need of treatment? Drug dependency is a family illness in a very real sense, but does that mean every family member is sick and that the overburdened taxpayer or premium payer should assume cost of care? Does this mean every mental health professional who discovers an alcoholic or addict in a patient's nuclear or extended family should expect to be reimbursed for treatment even if the identified alcoholic is miles away and not in treatment? Do we minimize the needs of the family members and, for financial reasons, refuse counseling and guidance even while we know it can lead to early identification of chemical dependency as the primary problem? Training families and others how to orchestrate an intervention brings reluctant addicts through the denial process and treatment long before they otherwise would be. Early treatment results in cost reduction, but insurance again remains a problem.

The 1980s also saw a surge in the movement to call attention to the special needs of the children of alcoholics, both the young and the adult. They are described as having unique problems, distinct from those even in children of other multiproblem families. Organizations were formed on both state and local levels to address their needs. A stated goal of at least one coalition for adult children of alcoholics was insurance coverage for their treatment. This led to more struggles between insurers and providers.

It is still too early to tell how much of this movement is fad and how much the wave of the future, much less what the real treatment needs may be. It is not too early, however, to foresee increased struggles over the limited treatment dollar. As those in need of chemical dependency treatment are defined in an ever-widening circle, other disciplines come forth to describe what that treatment should be and where it should be given. Extension of the term *addiction* to include all sorts of dependency may be an expensive ploy which could backfire. Nicotine, for example, is a highly addictive drug, but food and sex are needs of nature that require control by all people. Our profession must think twice about encouraging lawyers to use "sex addiction" and "food addiction" as defenses in criminal suits.

Treatment facilities have not always waited for answers and have adjusted their behavior to fiscal reality and opportunity. As a result, we now hear of more and more facilities that offer residential family treatment. At one treatment center, each family member was given a physical, a psychiatric diagnosis chosen from *DSM-III-R*, and a full medical record. Rates were the same as for the addicted family member. Such treatment was described not with apology but with an air of triumph. The payment system was outflanked, seemingly to everyone's profit.

As the 1990s approached, the notion of codependency broadened to include almost anyone who came from a dysfunctional family, whether or not alcohol or other drugs had played a significant role in that dysfunction. Now yet another group was invited into often very costly residential treatment, again under a psychiatric diagnosis.

Even if one does not object to this dishonesty per se and feels that civil disobedience or defiance of policy and procedure is justified if one is doing good for people, at least two long-term consequences followed. One was that the tremendous cost of family treatment provoked resentment and backlash so that other more appropriate treatment settings also risked being left uninsured. Most of the charts, lab tests, physical examinations, and other forms of overtreatment are not required. A hospital room is not needed for fully ambulatory people when a local motel offers rooms for much less than hospital rates. Less costly arrangements can be made even though the expenses will usually be only partially reimbursable.

Another hazard is that family members are given a psychiatric diagnosis and, whether or not the diagnosis is accurate, medical records are created for people, many of whom are still young and unaware of the implications. The day will certainly come when a person's medical record can be examined as part of a routine screening process or security check. It may include a psychiatric hospitalization dating from childhood or early adolescence and perhaps even others from various treatment facilities, if treatment was required more than once. How convincingly can people then explain that this was to ensure payment from an insurance company and that while frightened and upset, they really had not been mentally ill at all?

OVERTREATMENT AND UNDERTREATMENT

There are still wide variations among states in the amount of funds available for chemical dependency treatment. Some of these inflexible patterns force us to suggest treatment that we know is not well-suited to a patient's needs. Ideally, we want to have an entire spectrum of services from which to choose. That range might include outpatient care, social setting detoxification, halfway and quarterway houses, partial hospitalization, and short- and long-term residential care in freestanding or hospital-based settings. In many communities, only a few of these services exist. In others, only certain groups of insured people have financial access to them.

If a patient clearly requires removal from the home and a controlled, drug-free environment in which to recover, a hospital-based program may be the only alternative. While hospital-based programs often can and do give superb care, there is no question that they are expensive and, in many cases, necessary only because the less expensive alternatives are not available. Counselors who really do want to individualize treatment and select the appropriate level of care are caught between giving much too much and much too little. Because lives are at stake and because people are more valuable than dollars, there may be little choice other than to opt for overtreatment.

Not surprisingly, the 1980s also saw a rapid increase in HMOs, preferred-provider organizations, and managed care. Some of this resulted from the overall increase in health care costs. Some was a response to overcharging, greed, and the questionable business practices of hospitals, health care workers, and many chemical dependency treatment providers themselves.

Probably the most bothersome issues in our field today is that posed by managed care—called by some "managed costs" or "mismanaged care." Rather than blaming the HMOs, the insurance business, the greed of some treatment centers and private practitioners, or governmental bureaucracies—all of whom share some of the responsibility for the mess we are in—the most constructive approach seems to lie in cooperation between all these warring factions (Phillips 1984).

Taxpayers, premium payers, and insurers certainly all have a right to be concerned about cost containment. The profession has a legitimate concern about quality control and professional standards. And government at all levels has some responsibility for both. How to balance these sometimes competing interests is a formidable task. Turfdom and interprofessional animosity don't make it any easier.

The National Council on Alcoholism and Drug Dependence (NCADD) and other field organizations have made a very good point: clinical decisions are now being made by telephone, often by a clerk in an insurance company or a government office who may have little or no clinical training, experience, or knowledge of alcoholism and other addictions, and all of this without ever seeing the patient.

These decisions need not necessarily be made by a physician. In fact, in spite of the gratifying growth of the American Society of Addiction Medicine (ASAM), members of the medical profession, including deans of medical schools, admit that the average physician today still has less understanding of these problems and the patient's needs than a well-qualified professional addiction counselor or nurse-specialist. Decisions should, however, be made by someone knowledgeable about addiction medicine, someone whose performance is not measured primarily by the amount of treatment refused or money saved.

WHEN PROFIT IS KING

No institution that wants to be well regarded and accepted can do without paying attention to public relations. Referrals tend to come from friends, not strangers. Networks and linkages need care and attention if patients are to flow smoothly between the people who are responsible for their care.

People and organizations often send Christmas cards. The card may be replaced the following year by a calendar. Then the calendar may, in turn, be replaced by a modest gift like a memo pad holder or an inexpensive pen. At times the gift may become progressively more lavish. One EAP counselor who referred many patients to a particular facility received increasingly substantial gifts from them, until she received a very large cheese wheel complete with several sausages and tins of gourmet delicacies. Her statement at that time was "I'm beginning to feel bribed!"

Bribery has indeed entered the field. Empty beds are expensive. Expenses stay fairly static whether or not occupancy is good, but when only a few patients are in residence there is little income. With a few quick calculations the amount of money at stake becomes apparent. At $300 a day, keeping a single inpatient bed full all year would bring $109,500. For that kind of return it makes sense to recruit patients aggressively.

Some people with the power to send others to treatment may be well paid and unlikely to be tempted by invitations to make deals, but many others are not. While counselors working in employee assistance programs tend to earn respectable salaries, those in the not-for-profit sector are frequently underpaid, not only in dollars but in appreciation and recognition for the work they do. Many would love to do this work but feel they simply can't afford it.

It is not surprising then that alliances are formed that do not always work to the benefit of the patient. Outright payment for referrals does occur, and there are many subtle variations. One EAP counselor let it be known that he was available to lecture to patients in a New York City treatment facility for a fee. He added that he would find it convenient to lecture when he was escorting a patient to the facility for admission. Another described how he routinely drives his referrals to a New England facility where he is handsomely reimbursed for travel expenses, warmly received, and well fed.

The practice of trading favors, however, is fading. Facilities have their own marketing people and field representatives whose task is to create a demand for service and to ensure that patients choose to have their treatment with them. Television, radio, and print invite the patient to be evaluated and intimate that most insurance policies will cover treatment. There is nothing wrong with this if what is offered is honestly described and if the outcome of the initial evaluation has not been predetermined in such a way that the client with insurance inevitably ends up in residential treatment, irrespective of need.

The field representatives of treatment providers are expected to fill beds and keep up the census. If they do this successfully, they are well paid. If they fail, they are often out of work. They try to make contact with those who can refer large numbers of patients. They may also try to win the referent's loyalty to both the facility they represent and themselves, since many field representatives will change employers and gain substantial salary increases through the ability to take their contacts and following with them. This can be done simply on the basis of friendship. Sometimes the referral source believes the counselor's new facility is better than the former one and that the job change involved a desire to represent the place that does the best job for the patient. Sometimes it is. At other times the issues are financial.

Gifts and favors have sometimes been replaced by a bounty system in which money changes hands for every client successfully referred into treatment on a per capita basis. An extreme case in a western city involved an EAP counselor who was offered payment for each patient delivered as well as a full two-week vacation in the tropics if enough of his firm's employees could be persuaded to have their treatment in that hospital. More recently, a northern treatment facility arranged with two union-based counselors in the south to have all their referrals flown there for treatment.

In a society that is casual about accepting kickbacks and a variety of white-collar crimes, there is no reason to expect the addiction field to have escaped such problems. "Everybody's doing it!" is, however, simply untrue. Relatively few are doing it, and those who do are increasingly liable to be discovered. We have the integrity and the ability to keep dishonesty to a minimum, and we must learn to do so or patients will be hurt.

CHAPTER SIX
_____

PROFESSIONAL RELATIONS

The familiar question "Am I my brother's keeper?" appears in many contexts. People who have chosen careers in health care have already answered it affirmatively. Arguments arise as to how that must be done. No one can be accountable for everything and everyone, but neither can we hide behind the excuse that "It's not my job" when there is so much of importance that needs to be done.

OBLIGATIONS TO FAMILY AND COLLEAGUES

A good way to start sorting things out begins with knowing what each of us is qualified to do and what we can contribute. Obvious examples are obligations to one's own family—our responsibilities as parents, spouses, and siblings. These are tasks that can't be delegated to others. With the extended family of close friends and colleagues, there are similar concerns. They trust us to know them well and to be aware of signs of change or trouble long before outsiders would notice.

RESPECTING A.A. TRADITIONS

For many counselors, an even larger family than that of the workplace is the world of A.A. That remarkable organization asks little of its members in return for what it gives. It requires only that its customs and traditions be followed if its name is to be used. These guidelines keep A.A. intact as an organization so that it will remain available and effective for the generations to come (Maxwell 1984, Robertson 1988).

Counselors need to consider the short-term needs of their patients within the context of A.A.'s overall well-being. A.A. policies have been set only after considerable deliberation. There has been a great deal of grass-roots input through regional delegates as well as through the process of group conscience. Protecting A.A. or other Twelve Step groups, understanding them well, and presenting them fairly are important for both counselor and patient. It is beyond the scope of this discussion to do more than mention a few areas where problems arise.

Common problems include misunderstandings about anonymity. Unauthorized professionals may present themselves at media level as A.A. spokespersons. This implies that A.A. has endorsed or become affiliated with their particular treatment efforts or philosophy, actions that A.A. has always been extremely careful to avoid. Tapes have been made of A.A. talks, given at both outside meetings and in treatment facilities, which are then played for other groups without the speaker's knowledge or permission. A particularly striking case involved the use of a surgeon's A.A. personal story taped without her knowledge or permission and played for her medical students. An unthinking but well-meaning person thought that the students would be particularly interested in the experiences of a fellow physician. Indeed they were.

Although there is much overlap, the A.A. tradition of anonymity is not the same as the professional ethic of confidentiality. Both are concerned that the rights of the chemically dependent person, as well as the integrity of the entire chemical dependency field, be protected. The A.A. tradition of anonymity needs to be understood by both A.A. members and others who have any dealings with A.A. The A.A. tradition of anonymity is not intended to perpetuate the stigma of alcoholism, but to prevent ego trips among its members, to reassure newcomers who might fear for their reputations, and to protect the fellowship both from adverse publicity if a member relapses and from individuals appointing themselves spokespersons.

An A.A. pamphlet, *Understanding Anonymity*, based largely on the writings of cofounder Bill W., delineates a nice balance between grandiosity and the excessive secrecy which could prevent alcoholics from receiving the A.A. message. Traditions Eleven and Twelve forbid self-identification as an A.A. member through the media, while allowing one to identify oneself freely as an alcoholic. They forbid any unauthorized disclosure of another member's identity, but allow one to identify oneself as an A.A. member below the level of public media. Customs differ within the fellowship; some groups use only first names, yet full names are used within the majority of A.A. groups (some 80 percent of those attending one A.A. international convention).

A particularly tricky issue involves the attempt to get an A.A. group to undertake a reporting or monitoring function. Often a court or employer is willing to have an alcoholic attend A.A. meetings as a substitute for punishment or residential treatment, but evidence that attendance actually occurs is required. This poses no problem when the meetings are open and noses are not counted by the A.A. group itself. The difficulties arise if A.A. is presented to the newcomer as an extension of a coercive system that not only spies on members but reports back to others. Some problem drinkers who have been forced into A.A. closed meetings have no stake in refraining from gossip about those they see there. They also feel little or no responsibility for the smooth running of the meeting, nor do they feel a need to contribute anything more than their required physical presence.

Granted, some reluctant people do get exposed to A.A. in this fashion and many of them go on to become sober, active, and enthusiastic A.A. members. Others are taught that A.A. is just one more organization that may talk about anonymity and freedom of choice but is willing to join the establishment in coercing them. While some lives are doubtlessly saved by these tactics, other people are left with an experience that will prevent them from seeking A.A.'s help at a future time. There are other ways to establish attendance without having A.A. groups fill out chits or assume the role of police.

Alcoholics do not need new lessons in cynicism from the organization most deserving of their trust and confidence. It is easy to ask A.A. groups to fall into these traps, particularly if they are blackmailed with the threat that refusal may cost a fellow alcoholic his or her liberty. The long-range effects need to be considered and better methods must be devised. A.A. *Guidelines: Cooperating with Court, A.S.A.P., and Similar Programs* (Alcoholics Anonymous 1993) offers practical suggestions based on how these problems have been handled in some A.A. groups. These guidelines note that it is not the business of A.A. members to question what pressures from court, physician, spouse, or boss may have brought newcomers to A.A. (as they would have resented being so questioned when they came in), but to make the A.A. program attractive to those who do come.

Thoughtless referral practices have also caused trouble. One treatment center sent a whole busload of chemically dependent patients to a small-town A.A. meeting, overwhelming the group's total membership of eighteen. The treatment unit involved refused to stop the practice, so the A.A. group went underground, concealing both the time and site of its meetings.

In another city, a group of actively drinking young men who had been court-committed to a heroin treatment program were forced to attend A.A. They were disruptive, somewhat frightening to the members, and ultimately contributed to a backlash against drug-users that has caused friction within A.A. in many parts of the country.

When A.A. and other Twelve Step programs are treated with sophistication and their mores are understood and respected, counselors and groups can usually work out procedures that satisfy the needs of both parties. It is not fair for counselors to be so insistent on the particular needs of their own patients that they expect all rules to be broken in their behalf. The resulting upset and chaos can take many months to make right.

OBLIGATIONS TO THE COMMUNITY

Finally, we have obligations to the community at large. Those of us with special knowledge and expertise need to share it if others are to write and pass the laws that affect our present and future patients, as well as the countless others whom we will never personally know.

A.A., as an organization, quite wisely refrains from politics, neither endorses nor opposes any causes, and stays out of controversy. This has proved a wise policy, and the authors hope it continues. Individual A.A. members, on the other hand, may merely be uninterested or for other reasons may choose to hide behind the tradition of anonymity as an excuse for inaction. Others have sometimes confused what A.A. considers good policy for the organization (anonymity), with what they should do as individuals (advocacy).

Neither A.A. membership nor recovery from chemical dependency or any other illness should curtail the rights, privileges, or obligations of citizenship. Recovery is not just abstinence, even though abstinence must always come first. Participation in the world around us is part of recovery. To register and vote, to write to legislators, and to appear at public hearings are things we should do if we are to make our democracy work. For many of us, the authors included, this has meant learning about politics rather late in life, but learn we must. As members of NCADD with its network of local affiliates, of Employee Assistance Professionals Association, National Association of Social Workers, American Psychological Association, National Association of Alcoholism and Drug Abuse Counselors, American Society of Addiction Medicine, National Association of Addiction Treatment Providers and other professional and advocacy groups, many A.A. members do what they cannot do as members of A.A., and do so without violating anonymity. Bill W., Marty Mann, and Senator Harold E. Hughes all testified before Congress simply as alcoholics in recovery. Whether they were A.A. members wasn't mentioned, nor at the time was it pertinent.

If we do not take a hand in the political process, if people who are concerned with the well-being of those who are chemically dependent remain silent, others will continue to make important decisions for us. In the past, they have not always made these decisions wisely. And there are many decisions to be made: Are we to have warning, content, and ingredient labels on liquor bottles? What blood-alcohol level makes a driver intoxicated? Should people under age twenty-one be allowed to buy liquor, and should it be sold in drugstores and supermarkets? When federal money is divided between the needs of the chemically dependent and the mentally ill, how will the shares be allocated and how large will they be? Do we want insurance coverage for chemical dependency treatment? To whom, for what, and where shall it be given?

Our entire health care system will be undergoing major structural change now and in the years ahead, probably not in one vast upheaval but in a series of smaller changes, both nationally and state by state. Our professional organizations need to stay abreast of these changes, and when they ask us to back them with our own actions, we should.

Politicians are not interested in our personal histories, nor do they care whether or not we have recovered from chemical dependency. Like most people, their primary interest is in themselves. They want to know if we will vote for them, contribute to their campaigns, and get others to do the same. If they believe we will, they will pay attention to us. A surprisingly small effort can make a big difference in their actions. As long as we make an effort to be involved politically, we cannot be blamed for failing to make a difference. We will sometimes be ignored, but we can be blamed for not even trying.

OTHER PROFESSIONALS

A code of ethics is not complete without considering our obligation to respect other professionals and agencies. We may disagree with their philosophy or treatment methods, but unless these are downright harmful or malicious, professional courtesy requires us not to make unseemly comparisons. The chemical dependency field has been plagued with turf battles and jealous rivalry. This confuses patients and harms both the individual who stoops to this and our fledgling profession, which is struggling to gain public respect and find a place among the older professions. We look small when Treatment Center A gloats over its success with Treatment Center B's failures, while over at Treatment Center B the converse is happening.

One chairman of the A.A. General Service Board has stated, "Progress in this field will be made in direct proportion to the degree of respect and cooperation between A.A. and the treatment facilities." This is fully consonant with the history of A.A. as seen in the book *Alcoholics Anonymous Comes of Age,* and with A.A.'s stated intent not to oppose or endorse any causes (the A.A. Preamble and Traditions Six and Ten).

False and misleading advertising is both illegal and unethical. Advertising by treatment agencies, properly done, can benefit the public by removing the stigma of the disease, emphasizing that it is treatable, breaking down denial, and letting victims know help is available. But abuses can creep in. The advertising code of the National Association of Addiction Treatment Providers says that advertising should emphasize the desirability of treatment without referring to specific and/or absolute percentages of recovery, and should not imply that recovery is "patently simple, comfortable, or effortless" (NAATP 1982).

The NAATP code forbids self-promotion through negative implications about competitors. Clearly unethical, in the authors' opinion, is the policy of one group that promotes itself largely by derogatory and often false statements about A.A., for example, that it is a religion (A.A. meets none of the major elements of the accepted definition and welcomes atheists and agnostics), and that it fosters overdependence (on the contrary, A.A. is a program of self-growth among peers, healthier than dependence on therapists). Furthermore, the "powerlessness" this group criticizes actually gives alcoholics freedom to choose not to drink instead of slavery to the bottle.

The real conflicts arise when we become aware that a person or an institution gives poor care or exploits or endangers patients. Do we sound the alarm or look the other way? Can a way be found to promote change?

A profession is supposed to be self-regulating, acting from professional integrity rather than fear of prosecution or lawsuits. Most professional organizations have ethics committees or conduct review boards, and members are expected to inform them of unethical conduct. This is not mere tattling or gossip but the way in which a profession gains respect and trust. Intervention with a colleague is aimed at being helpful, not vindictive. The danger of an incompetent worker harming clients must be averted.

If concern for peers is a hallmark of the professional, we need to be aware of one another and be ready to reach out in times of trouble. This can be an obvious action like helping someone through a bout of serious physical illness, divorce, or a family crisis. It can be more difficult if a colleague relapses into drinking, experiences emotional illness, or acts unethically putting patients at risk. No one wants to be seen as intrusive, prudish, or judgmental, and no one enjoys confronting a friend. Just as members of nuclear families may compound their problems by enabling or covering up for each other, so too can treatment staff.

For similar reasons, recommendations for employment must be honest and not reflect the good-old-boy syndrome. Qualifications should be carefully checked. In one instance, an applicant gave the impression that he had completed a certain training program when he had actually received a D in the basic course and dropped out. "Clean" drug counselors have been found to be active alcoholics.

PUBLICATION AND PUBLIC SPEAKING

The ethics of publication are too often violated in the addiction field, where the copy machine too often engenders a failure to respect the rights of authors and publishers to their just earnings. This is stealing and a violation of U.S. copyright laws. Plagiarism involves the borrowing of another's material, copyrighted or not, without proper permission or printed acknowledgment of the source.

An increasing problem is that created by the easy availability of audiotapes. Speakers are often not asked if they object to being taped. Their remarks have later been known to appear verbatim over someone else's byline. Others who have agreed to share personal stories with a particular audience find that tapes have been made, sold, or shared, without their permission. Some of the worst offenders have been A.A. and other Twelve Step group members who might not gossip or reveal the full name of a fellow home group member but assume that anyone who agrees to be a speaker at a larger gathering has renounced the right to anonymity.

Most of these problems can be avoided if expectations are made clear in advance. If speakers at a conference will be audiotaped or videotaped, they have a right to know that before they agree to the engagement. If a paper will be expected or remarks printed as part of the event's proceedings, that too should be understood.

If the speaker is to be paid, financial arrangements should be clear and these obligations met promptly. One of the reasons a doctor wears a hood along with his or her graduation gown is that the doctor's hood used to provide a place where fees could be discreetly tucked at the end of a visit to a patient. Neither party then had to face the indelicate problem of discussing money. Some people may still feel uncomfortable discussing monetary compensation. Nevertheless, we owe our fellow professionals a fair fee for their time and talent and, if we cannot manage this, they must be told. They may choose to donate their time, but they deserve to know if that is what is being asked. Even if the professional fee is waived, courtesy and consideration demand that travel and other expenses be reimbursed.

Conversely, employees have ethical obligations to the institution that employs them. Employees may sometimes need to challenge its policies to serve the patients' best interests, but if this is not the case, one should be loyal or look for another position. Respect for institutional policies and management functions is essential for the serenity of all who work there. It is important to learn how to work through channels of authority in order to effect change, instead of undermining or misrepresenting an immediate superior. In general it is more constructive to work through the chain of command—to complain to the director, not to members of the board, unless it is a question of the board removing the director.

Professionals must always be conscious of the difference between speaking as individuals and speaking as representatives of a professional group or agency. Speakers must realize that their position and obligation to others may, at times, severely limit freedom of speech. Lying isn't necessary but there are times to step aside and let someone else be the speaker.

OBLIGATIONS OF ANIMAL RESEARCHERS

The ethics of using animals for scientific experimentation has received thorough treatment from both the AMA and the APA; both insist on taking all *reasonable* precautions to ensure animals are not abused or made to suffer. Certainly they should not be used when nonliving substitutes are available or when the knowledge gained will be trivial. Some arguments based on the rights of animals as living beings would logically make the entire food chain immoral. The search for the cure of a major illness is not the same as creating a new cosmetic. Our obligation of humane behavior toward animals stems from our status as moral individuals and stewards of lower creatures. Abuse of animals is a violation of our human nature, not of animal "rights."

CHAPTER SEVEN

CONCLUSION

The chemical dependency counselor, whether from another health care profession or from this new profession only, can expect to face all the dilemmas faced over the years by caregivers from other disciplines. Threats, offers of bribes, and the temptation to compromise one's standards are part of human history. In every age and in every country, some agree and some refuse. Cynics may say, "Everyone has a price." Perhaps, but the authors hope not. We all have different standards and feelings about where each of us must draw the line if we are to live comfortably with ourselves and sleep soundly at night.

Some behavior is so clearly unethical and unacceptable it requires no discussion. Other actions lie in the gray areas where rationalization can make questionable practices seem all right if they are not examined too closely. Sometimes these are, indeed, all right when seen in full context.

These questions are not the only ones that are important in thinking about our ethics as counselors. New ones arise and old ones change. We are often still groping for many of the answers, but we can at least not be naïve or unthinking, and not be surprised or indignant when we see, far too late, what was under our nose had we been willing to look. When considering the ethics of a given situation, we would do well to keep it simple, to think first of the patient, and to ask, What is my professional, ethical duty toward this patient? It may also help to ask, What would I want for myself or for someone important to me if I were in this person's place?

Professional ethics have a deeper basis for right and wrong than fear of being arrested or sued. Some legal actions are unethical, some ethical actions are illegal. Just because we are threatened with a lawsuit does not mean we are wrong or will lose, but even good people and their colleagues can be successfully sued if they leave themselves liable. We need to reduce liability by reasonably reducing the risk of accidents or incompetent service, and by recording the remedies we adopt so that evidence can be produced in court.

Until the current liability crisis is resolved through tort reform or other legislation, we may let the fear of litigation determine our actions. Doctors often order unneeded and expensive tests and procedures for fear of being sued if they don't. Drugs and devices are being withdrawn from the market because it is impossible to guarantee there will be no side effects. Cases are multiplying where the same physician has been sued, sometimes successfully, for handling similar cases in exactly opposite ways: these are ethical, competent practitioners who were wrong legally no matter which way they acted.

It is impossible to avoid litigation altogether. Fear of litigation can easily distort our judgment and sense of what is right or wrong. There will be times when we must do what we believe is honest and ethical, no matter how it may appear in a court of law. If we carefully record what we have done and the thinking that supports our decision, the consequences are usually acceptable. Trouble is predictable when we appear to be careless or malicious, alter records, or seem to make excuses. We need not all be exemplary lawbreakers like the saints and prophets of major religions, but there will be times when legal justice conflicts with right and wrong. Then each of us must choose a course of action known in advance to be a "no win."

CODE OF ETHICS

Every code of ethics borrows from what others have done. Each code tries to reflect the particular profession's individual needs, and several codes have been developed for the addiction field; for example, by the American Society of Addiction Medicine (ASAM) in 1992, and by the National Association of Alcoholism and Drug Abuse Counselors (NAADAC 1987, 1990; also Madden and Offenberg 1979, Staub and Kent 1973, Valle 1979). The one offered below was initially borrowed from another source, then further developed in two different residential treatment centers, then modified again after consideration of ASAM's code. It should not be regarded as finished, nor is it presented as a model. It does reflect the efforts of a number of concerned people to reach some sort of agreement about how we, as professionals in the addiction field, can conduct ourselves as we work together. It will provide a starting point.

STAFF CODE OF ETHICS

1. As a member of the GREATPLACE professional staff or member of its board of directors, I will place the welfare of our patients and their families in matters affecting them above all other concerns.

2. To this end, I will deliver kind and humane treatment to all in my care regardless of race, creed, reproductive status, sex, disability, age, or sexual orientation.

3. I will not deliberately do harm to a patient, either physically or psychologically. I will not verbally assault, ridicule, attempt to subjugate, or endanger a patient, nor will I allow other patients or staff to do so.

4. I will urge changes in the lives of patients only in their behalf and in the interest of promoting recovery from the illness we are charged to treat. I will not otherwise press them to adopt beliefs and behaviors that reflect my value system rather than their own.

5. I will remain aware of my own skills and limitations. Since patients and former patients may perceive me as an authority and hence overvalue my opinions, I will attempt never to counsel or advise them on matters not within my area of expertise. I will be willing to recognize when it is in the best interest of my patients to release or refer them to another program or individual.

6. I will not engage in any activity that could be construed as exploitation of patients for personal gain, be it sexual, financial, or social.

7. I will not attempt to use my authority over a patient in a coercive manner to meet my own ends. I will not promote dependence on me, but help patients to empower themselves.

8. I will not name or give information about a patient, former patient, or family member except to other GREATPLACE staff as required by treatment or when specifically authorized by the patient.

9. I understand and agree to defend both the spirit and the letter of GREATPLACE policy on patient rights and the patient's bill of rights, and to respect the rights and views of other professionals.

10. As a caring and caregiving person, I understand that a therapeutic relationship does not end with a person's leaving GREATPLACE. I will recognize the need to conduct any subsequent relationships with former patients with the same concern for their well-being that is acknowledged above. Sexual involvement with a patient is unethical. Sexual involvement with a former patient exploits emotions deriving from treatment and is therefore almost always unethical.

11. In my personal use of alcohol and other mood-altering drugs, I will serve as a responsible role model for patients,

staff, and community. If I have been chemically dependent in the past, I will maintain total abstinence while employed at GREATPLACE.

12. I will exhibit responsible concern for the well-being of my peers and the GREATPLACE community by not ignoring manifestations of illness or unethical conduct in colleagues.

13. I will accept responsibility for my continuing education and professional development as part of my commitment to providing quality care for those who seek my help.

CASE STUDIES IN ETHICS FOR ADDICTION COUNSELORS

These are all actual cases. Details have been modified to avoid identification of individuals. Answers should be based on such questions as *What rights are involved? Whose rights take priority? Why? What values are at stake?*

1. You are a certified addiction counselor in private practice. A client comes for assessment of her son. You see a complex mother-child conflict and warn her that the assessment may take four hours, including a test. She later complains to another professional that you have overcharged her. He agrees with her and says it should not have taken that long. How do you handle it? Did the other professional act unethically?

2. Treatment Center X offers to pay a fee directly to an intervention specialist. The interventionist refuses, saying she considers this unethical, a conflict of interest, but if the treatment center wishes to reimburse the family for up to four hundred dollars of her fee, the family would be responsible for the balance. Who is right: the interventionist or the treatment center? Why?

3. There is only one treatment center exclusively for women in the state, headed by a fully qualified and certified woman addictions counselor, also certified as a nurse addiction specialist. A major insurance company refuses to refer women to her because she is not a licensed psychologist or medical doctor. Is the insurance company's action ethical?

4. An interventionist refers an *overtly* suicidal alcoholic and three-time loser in standard alcoholism treatment programs to a ninety-day residential center with excellent psychiatric staff specializing in dual diagnosis cases. The alcoholism treatment center to which the interventionist usually referred patients complained that he was violating their tacit agreement. Did the center act professionally?

5. An addicted patient's insurance coverage is running out. His withdrawal is over, but he complains of a depression, which is probably just typical of that stage. Your supervisor tells you to change the diagnosis to clinical depression so medical insurance will cover continued stay in treatment. What should you do?

6. I am a treatment center counselor and a member of A.A. At an A.A. meeting in my community, I notice that Geneva, a patient from my treatment center, is also in attendance. The patient talks in the meeting about having had a relapse the previous weekend. I realize she has not talked about her relapse in her outpatient treatment group, although patients are encouraged to do so in the interest of their own recovery processes. What should I do, if anything?

7. Another patient tells you that in the A.A. group he attends there is a man who mentioned committing a felony, embezzlement, for which he was never caught. He asks you if he has an obligation to the company that was embezzled to

report this, since there is no law of confidentiality that binds him as an A.A. member. What is your answer?

8. Matilda M. is a patient on your treatment center caseload. She has a seizure disorder and has been told by her physician that she must take Dilantin, an anticonvulsant, to prevent further seizures. Her A.A. sponsor has told her she has to change her sobriety date because "You can't be sober and be on other drugs." How do you respond to Matilda?

9. Your patient Mary introduced herself on a television program with the statement, "I'm Mary Brown, and I'm an alcoholic." Now she worries that she has violated the A.A. tradition of anonymity. What do you say?

10. Dagwood B., a client of yours, says he hates the meeting at 12th and Elm. What is your response?

11. Dagwood B. also complains about "all the God talk" saying he is an agnostic and does not buy any religion. Again, what do you say?

12. You are the EAP counselor in a firm. An alcoholic employee whom you have been counseling—now in early sobriety—admits to you he has been embezzling large sums of money from the firm. You are a trusted employee of the firm. Must you inform them? May you? What should you do?

13. A recovering patient has made good progress, and it is clear she no longer needs your counseling. You want to terminate her, but your supervisor says that since her insurance is covering her bills, you should continue treatment to help pay for some of the charity cases the agency has. What should you do?

14. A young chemical dependency counselor trainee in an inpatient center is heard making a sexual remark to a female patient. The training supervisor fires him on the

spot. He appeals to you, the administrator. Do you back the supervisor? How do you handle it?

15. Two years of continual sobriety is a condition for certification as a chemical dependency counselor in your state. A colleague, a recovered alcoholic with five years of sobriety and a certified counselor working in the field, relapses. You are the only one who knows, but not through any confidential communication from him nor anyone else. Is there an impaired counselor program in your state? If so, should you report this? If not, should you organize an intervention team? What should you do? What if this was a brief episode, now apparently ended?

16. You are an addiction counselor in an outpatient setting. A client you have been counseling, apparently with good progress, does not tell you she has recently started seeing a clinical psychologist. You find out indirectly but ethically. What do you do or say?

17. Susie is an attractive woman whom you have counseled at your inpatient treatment program. You have been careful not to exploit the relationship in spite of the fact that she has exhibited transference of positive feelings toward you. She has now been out of treatment and sober for over a year. You meet at an A.A. meeting and she asks you to be her sponsor. Is this okay? Then she asks you to meet for dinner before an A.A. meeting. Is this okay? There is a dance after the meeting. After the dance she asks if you would like to go to her apartment. Is this okay? What principles or guidelines are applicable here?

18. A high-ranking member of the clergy tests positive for HIV. He has fathered several children and expects to continue doing so. He refuses to tell his wife about the test results. As a professional, what do you do? (So far, the cleric's state has

no mandatory reporting law.) How do you balance his right to privacy and confidentiality, and his genuine fear of serious repercussions if the full story comes out, against his wife's right to health for herself and the children to come?

19. You are a consultant to a firm whose president entrusts to you a company secret. She knows you usually share all such information with your partner, an old and trusted friend. This time she says you may not share it with your partner. When the news breaks, your partner accuses you of disloyalty; he insists you had a prior obligation to tell him in spite of the president's wish that you not share this particular bit of information. Did you act correctly or is your partner right?

20. A female counselor advised divorce for a couple, then married the husband. The wife sued her. Was the counselor ethical?

21. An alcoholic patient recovering in your treatment center admits to sexually abusing and beating his child. State law requires that child abuse be reported to a state agency, even if known via a confidential relationship. Federal law prohibits identifying the patient as even being in your center. What should you do?

BIBLIOGRAPHY

While there is a vast literature on general ethics and a growing mass of publications on ethics for various professions, such as medicine, nursing, social work, psychology, law, business and engineering, there is relatively little which is specific to the ethics of addiction professionals. We have not attempted to list all the current material on professional ethics, or even to select the best. What follows are representative titles, along with those specific to the chemical dependency profession.

Ethical/Legal Dilemmas. 1992. *Addiction & Recovery*. 12(7): 5-10.

Al-Anon Family Group Headquarters, Inc. 1987. *Al-Anon and Professionals* (formerly titled *Working As, For, or With Professionals*). New York: Al-Anon Family Group.

Alcoholics Anonymous World Services, Inc. 1972. *If You Are a Professional, A.A. Wants to Work with You*. New York: Alcoholics Anonymous World Services.

———. 1974. *How A.A. Members Cooperate with Other Community Efforts to Help Alcoholics*. New York: Alcoholics Anonymous World Services.

———. 1975. *Three Talks to Medical Societies, by Bill W., Co-founder of A.A.* New York: Alcoholics Anonymous World Services.

———. 1982. *A.A. as a Resource for the Medical Profession*. New York: Alcoholics Anonymous World Services.

———. 1993. A.A. Guidelines: For A.A. Members Employed in the Alcoholism Field (formerly subtitled For Those Who Wear Two Hats). New York: A.A. General Service Office.

———. 1993. A.A. Guidelines: Cooperating with Court, A.S.A.P. and Similar Programs. New York: A.A. General Service Office.

American Psychological Association. 1981. Ethical Principles of Psychologists. Washington, D.C.: APA. First published in American Psychologist 36: 633-638.

Andrews, Lewis M. 1987. Beyond Addiction. Chapter 12 in To Thine Own Self Be True: The Rebirth of Values in the New Ethical Therapy. New York: Anchor Press/Doubleday.

Apthorp, Stephen P. 1985. Alcohol and Substance Abuse: A Clergy Handbook. Wilton, Conn.: Morehouse-Barlow.

Ashley, Benedict M., and Kevin O'Rourke. 1986. The Ethics of Health Care. St. Louis, Mo.: Catholic Health Association.

Beauchamp, Tom L., and James F. Childress. 1983. Principles of Biomedical Ethics. 2d ed. New York: Oxford University Press.

Birch & Davis Associates. 1986. Development of Model Professional Standards for Alcoholism Counselor Credentialing. Arlington, Va.: National Association of Alcoholism and Drug Abuse Counselors.

Bissell, LeClair, and Paul Haberman. 1984. Alcoholism in the Professions. New York: Oxford University Press.

Blume, Sheila B. 1977. Ethics of Record-Keeping. Alcoholism: Clinical and Experimental Research 1(4): 301-303.

———. 1987. Confidentiality of Medical Records in Alcohol-Related Problems. New York: National Council on Alcoholism.

Brown, Stephanie. 1985. Treating the Alcoholic. New York: Wiley. (Shows how A.A. and psychotherapy can cooperate.)

Carroll, Mary Ann, H. G. Schneider, and G. R. Wesley. 1985. Ethics in the Practice of Psychology. Englewood, N.J.: Prentice-Hall.

Confidentiality of Alcohol and Drug Abuse Patient Records. 1975. Federal Register 40(127), Pt. 4: 27802-21.

Confidentiality of Alcohol and Drug Abuse Patient Records. 1982. *Code of Federal Regulations* Title 42, Pt. 2.

Corey, Gerald, ed. 1986. *Theory and Practice of Counseling and Psychotherapy*, Monterey, Calif.: Brooks-Cole. (See especially chapter 13.)

Corey, Gerald, Marianne S. Corey, and P. Callahan. 1988. *Issues and Ethics in the Helping Professions*. Monterey, Calif.: Brooks-Cole.

Evans, David S. 1990. Confidentiality. *Addiction and Recovery* 10(2): 17-18.

Fagothey, Austin. 1976. *Right and Reason*. 6th ed. St. Louis, Mo.: C. V. Mosby. (Excellent for general ethical principles.)

Finnegan, Dana, and Emily McNally. 1987. *Dual Identities: Counseling Chemically Dependent Gay Men and Lesbians*. Center City, Minn.: Hazelden Educational Materials.

Gardner, Richard A. 1991. *True and False Accusations of Child Abuse*. Creskill, N.J.: Creative Therapeutics.

Gartrell, Nanette, et al. 1986. Psychiatrist-Patient Sexual Contact: Results of a National Survey, I: Prevalence. *American Journal of Psychiatry* 143:1126-1131.

Gazda, George M. 1978. Chapters 10 and 12 in *Group Counseling: A Developmental Approach*. 2d ed. Boston, Mass.: Allyn & Bacon.

Gill, James J., F. J. Braceland, et al. 1979. Ethics and Psychiatry. *Psychiatric Annals* 9(2): entire issue.

Goldberg, Raymond. 1993. *Taking Sides: Clashing Views on Controversial Issues in Drugs and Society*. Guilford, Conn.: Dushkin Publishing Group.

Gonsalves, Milton A. 1985. *Fagothey's Right and Reason: Ethics, Theory and Practice*. 8th ed. St. Louis, Mo.: Times Mirror/Mosby.

Gosselin, Renee, and Suzanne Nice. 1987. *Lesbian and Gay Issues in Early Recovery*. Center City, Minn.: Hazelden Educational Materials.

Greenberg, A. 1992. Working with Families of Mentally Ill Chemical Abusers. *Professional Counselor* 7(2): 45-51.

Gregson, D., and H. Summers. 1992. 13th Stepping: Young Women at Risk in AA and NA. *Professional Counselor* 7(2): 33-7.

Halleck, S. L. 1971. *The Politics of Therapy*. New York: Science House.

Hannah, Gerald T., et al., eds. 1982. *Preservation of Client Rights*. New York: Free Press/Macmillan.

Hazelden Evaluation Consortium. 1986. *Treatment Benchmarks*. Center City, Minn.: Hazelden Educational Materials.

Hummel, Dean L., et al. 1987. *Law and Ethics in Counseling*. Florence, Ky.: Van Nostrand Reinhold.

Jones, Donald G., ed. 1978. *Private and Public Ethics*. New York: Edwin Mellen Press.

Journal of Medical Humanities and Bioethics (formerly *Journal of Bioethics*). 1982—. New York: Human Sciences Press.

Keith-Spiegel, Patricia, and G. P. Koocher. 1985. *Ethics in Psychology: Professional Standards and Cases*. New York: Random House.

Keller, Mark. 1975. Multidisciplinary Perspectives on Alcoholism and the Need for Integration: A Historical and Prospective Note. *Journal of Studies on Alcohol* 36: 133-147.

King, Bruce. 1983. Betraying the Alcoholic or Protecting the Child? The Dilemma of Confidentiality. *Alcoholism: The National Magazine* 3(7): 59-61.

Knapp, Samuel, and Leon Vandecreek. 1987. *Privileged Communications in the Mental Health Professions*. Florence, Ky.: Van Nostrand Reinhold.

Koop, C. Everett. 1986. From the Surgeon General: Surgeon General's Report on Acquired Immune Deficiency Syndrome. *Journal of the American Medical Association* 256(20): 2783-2789.

Krystal, H., and R. A. Moore. 1963. Who is Qualified to Treat the Alcoholic? A Discussion. *Quarterly Journal of Studies on Alcohol* 24: 705-720. (Also see Lemere, below.)

Lawson, Gary, D. C. Ellis, and P. C. Rivers. 1984. Chapters 6 and 7 in *Essentials of Chemical Dependency Counseling*. Rockville, Md.: Aspen Publications.

Lemere, Frederick. 1964. Who is Qualified to Treat the Alcoholic? Comment on the Krystal-Moore Discussion. *Quarterly Journal of Studies on Alcohol* 25: 558-560.

Lewis, Jay, ed. 1983. *The Alcoholism Report* 11: 8.

MacIntyre, Alasdair. 1984. *After Virtue: A Study in Moral Theory*. 2d ed. Notre Dame, Ind.: Notre Dame Press.

Madden, Elaine, and Donald Offenberg, eds. 1979. *Ethical Issues in Substance Abuse Treatment*. Eagleville, Penn.: Eagleville Hospital and Rehabilitation Center.

Margolin, Gayla. 1982. Ethical and Legal Considerations in Marital and Family Therapy. *American Psychologist* 37(7): 788-801.

Maxwell, Milton. 1984. *The A.A. Experience: A Close-up View for Professionals*. New York: McGraw-Hill.

Monagle, John F., and David C. Thomasma. 1987. *Medical Ethics: A Guide for Health Care Professionals*. Florence, Ky.: Van Nostrand Reinhold.

National Association of Alcoholism and Drug Abuse Counselors (NAADAC). 1987. NAADAC Code of Ethics. *The Counselor*. 5(September/October): 13-16. Also published as *Code of Ethics*. Arlington, Va.: National Association of Alcoholism and Drug Abuse Counselors.

———. 1990. National Understanding of the NAADAC Code of Ethics, by Thomas F. McGovern, Lloyd Wright, and Nina Manley Wright. *The Counselor* 8(May/June): 37-8.

National Association of Addiction Treatment Providers (NAATP). 1982. *Advertising Code for Alcoholism Treatment Programs*, addition to their *Principles of Practice*. Irvine, Calif.: National Association of Addiction Treatment Providers.

National Institute on Alcohol Abuse and Alcoholism (NIAAA). 1979. Confidentiality of Alcohol and Drug Abuse Records and Child Abuse and Neglect Reporting. *Alcohol Health and Research World* 4(1): 31-4.

———. 1991. Linking Alcoholism Treatment Research with Clinical Practice. *Alcohol Health and Research World* 15(3): entire issue. (See especially the articles by Archer, McCrady, Geller, Huey.)

Nye, Sandra G., and Laura B. Kaiser. 1990. *Employee Assistance Law Answer Book*. New York: Panel Publishers.

———. 1992. *Employee Assistance Law Answer Book: 1992 Supplement*. New York: Panel Publishers.

Peterson, Marilyn R. 1992. *At Personal Risk: Boundary Violations in Professional-Client Relationships*. New York: Norton.

Phillips, Donald A. 1984. An Impossible Dream and a Little Outrage. Parts 1 and 2. *The Almacan* 14(September): 6, 18-19; 14(October): 6-7, 16. (Discusses EAPs and health care systems.)

Powell, David J. 1988. Clinical Supervision: The Missing Puzzle Piece. *The Counselor* 6(May/June): 20-22.

Program Information Associates. 1985. *The Counselor's Guide to Confidentiality*. Honolulu, Hawaii: PIA.

Pryzwansky, Walter B., and Robert N. Wendt. 1987. *Psychology as a Profession: Foundations of Practice*. New York: Pergamon Books.

Reamer, Frederic G. 1982. *Ethical Dilemmas in Social Service*. New York: Columbia University Press.

Robertson, Nan. 1988. *Getting Sober: Inside Alcoholics Anonymous*. New York: Morrow.

Royce, James E. 1986. Recovered vs. Recovering: What's the Difference? *U.S. Journal of Drug and Alcohol Dependence* 10(3): 7.

———. 1989. Chapters 19 and 21 in *Alcohol Problems and Alcoholism*. rev. ed. New York: Free Press/Macmillan.

Rutter, Peter. 1989. *Sex in the Forbidden Zone*. Los Angeles: J. P. Tarcher.

Schoener, Gary R., et al. 1989. *Psychotherapists' Sexual Involvement with Clients—Intervention and Prevention*. Minneapolis: Walk-In Counseling Center.

Staub, George, and L. Kent, eds. 1973. *The Para-Professional in the Treatment of Alcoholism: A New Profession*. Springfield, Ill.: Charles C. Thomas.

Thompson, Andrew. 1983. *Ethical Concerns in Psychotherapy and Their Legal Implications*. Lantham, Md.: University Press of America.

Tyrrell, Bernard J. 1975. *Christotherapy I*. New York: Paulist Press.

———. 1982. *Christotherapy II*. New York: Paulist Press.

Valle, Stephen. 1979. *Alcoholism Counseling: Issues for an Emerging Profession*. Springfield, Ill.: Charles C. Thomas.

Van Hoose, William H., and J. A. Kottler. 1985. *Ethical and Legal Issues in Counseling and Psychotherapy*. 2d ed. San Francisco, Calif.: Josey-Bass.

West, Judith M. 1988. Ethics and the Impaired Counselor. *The Counselor* 6 (November/December): 2, 37. (Self-assessment)

———. *Ethics in Counseling*. Audiotapes. NAADAC Tapes, Arlington, VA 22204.

White, William L. 1992. *Critical Incidents*. Bloomington, Ill.: Lighthouse Training Institute.

Wilson, James Q. 1993. *The Moral Sense*. New York: Macmillan/Free Press.

INDEX

More titles of interest . . .

Treating Coexisting Psychiatric and Addictive Disorders
A Practical Guide
edited by Norman S. Miller, M.D.
Focusing on the provision of treatment—not etiology or diagnosis—this book offers the thinking of many professionals on a broad range of dual diagnosis issues. Topics include case management and dual diagnosis, managed care and dual diagnosis, medications used with the dually diagnosed, and many more. 272 pp.
Order No. 1499

The Minnesota Model
The Evolution of the Multidisciplinary Approach to Addiction Recovery
by Jerry Spicer, M.H.A.
This book explores the Minnesota Model—a unique blend of behavioral science and A.A. principles that forms an effective, humane way to treat chemical dependency. Hazelden President Jerry Spicer takes an inside look at the model: how it began, how it works, and what's in store for the future. 178 pp.
Order No. 5148

Dual Disorders—Second Edition
Counseling Clients with Chemical Dependency and Mental Illness
by Dennis C. Daley, M.S.W., Howard B. Moss, M.D., and Frances Campbell, M.S.N.
This updated book is a practical, must-read resource for mental health and chemical dependency counselors. Focusing on educational, cognitive, and behavioral interventions for clients with dual disorders and their families, this guide provides a host of ideas on how to better serve this growing population. 250 pp.
Order No. 5023

**For price and order information, or a free catalog,
please call our Telephone Representatives.**

HAZELDEN EDUCATIONAL MATERIALS

1-800-328-9000	**1-612-257-4010**	**1-612-257-1331**
(Toll Free. U.S., Canada, and the Virgin Islands)	(Outside the U.S. and Canada)	(24-Hour FAX)

Pleasant Valley Road • P.O. Box 176 • Center City, MN 55012-0176